WRITING FOR THE MEDIA

PRCA PRACTICE GUIDES

WRITING FOR THE MEDIA

BY

ADRIAN WHEELER

FPRCA

emerald PUBLISHING

United Kingdom – North America – Japan – India
Malaysia – China

Emerald Publishing Limited
Howard House, Wagon Lane, Bingley BD16 1WA, UK

First edition 2019

British Library Cataloguing in Publication Data
A catalogue record for this book is available from the British Library

ISBN: 978-1-78756-614-9 (Print)
ISBN: 978-1-78756-611-8 (E-ISBN)
ISBN: 978-1-78756-613-2 (Epub)

ISOQAR
REGISTERED
Certificate Number 1985
ISO 14001

ISOQAR certified Management System, awarded to Emerald for adherence to Environmental standard ISO 14001:2004.

INVESTOR IN PEOPLE

CONTENTS

FOREWORD

PRCA Practice Guides are a series of uniquely practical and readable guides, providing public relations (PR) and communications professionals, new and experienced alike, with hands-on guidance to manage in the field. Written by experienced practitioners who have been there and done it, the books in this series offer powerful insights into the challenges of the modern industry and guidance on how to navigate your way through them.

This book sets out to help PR and communications get better results from their media relations, including a better profile in the media, and more pieces of press coverage that reflect positively on your organisation or client. In 1924, Basil Clarke, one of the first PR practitioners, said: '99 per cent of the copy sent to newspapers is doomed to the waste-basket'. Ninety years later Anthony Hilton, a distinguished and popular City Editor, said: 'The trick is to find the one release in a hundred which has something interesting to say'. Nobody wants to accept a hit rate of one per cent, and nobody needs to. Successful media programmes depend on three factors: knowing the media and knowing a lot about them; never issuing a 'story' which isn't really a story; and writing in a manner which the media appreciate. It is the third of these factors which this book addresses. Journalists are taught to construct stories and write English in a particular way; PR people, in general, are not. Learning how to emulate the media's own rules and style has an immeasurable effect on take-up.

The book is meant to be used as a practical guide and it contains numerous examples, checklists and quotes from eminent journalists.

Adrian Wheeler started out as a local newspaper reporter before training at a financial PR firm in the City. He co-founded Sterling Public Relations, a general practice agency, in 1976. This firm became the UK office of GCI Europe. As Chief Executive Officer of GCI UK, Wheeler led the company into the UK Top Ten and in 2000 and as Chairman of GCI Europe, he oversaw the development of a 28-office network with 53 multi-country clients. Since 2006 he has been a Partner in Agincourt Communications and a Non-executive Director at Liquid, London Communications Agency and Best Communications in Prague. He is a Fellow of the PRCA and a PR trainer who teaches clients and consultancies throughout Europe and the Middle East.

Francis Ingham
Director General, PRCA
Chief Executive, ICCO

ACKNOWLEDGEMENT

I would like to thank Isabella Ross for her help in reviewing the draft of this book and contributing many valuable suggestions.

INTRODUCTION

We have clients and employers (who pay us) and 'customers' (who don't). Our customers are the media: reporters, journalists, editors and publishers who decide our fate; if they use the material we offer them, our clients and employers will be pleased. If not, we will face a competitive review or a career appraisal sooner or later.

We all know that PR professionals perform a host of services which are nothing to do with the media. But most of us, most of the time, devote 60 per cent of our working hours to media engagement ... writing material and trying to place it in media outlets which will make a difference to our clients' or employers' success.

Ten years ago there were 70,000 people working in the UK media and 30,000 of us. Now there are 23,000 employed in the media and 86,000 of us. Nick Davies has calculated that over 90 per cent of the material on TV, radio and mainstream news brands comes from PR departments and agencies (Davies, 2008).

Some of the people working in PR used to work in the media. The most eminent example is probably Colin Byrne, who retired from Weber Shandwick in March 2018. The least eminent is probably myself, who worked on the UK's first freesheet before turning to PR. But both of us, and hundreds of others, had the opportunity to learn the media's rules and conventions before we switched to public relations.

It matters. If you know how to produce material that complies with the media's own customs, your hit-rate rises dramatically. The media no longer have time to re-write and call to fill in the gaps. Unless you're Apple, Google or Trump, it makes sense to get it right first time.

The aim of this PRCA Practice Guide is to help PR people who *didn't* work in the media know more about the criteria journalists and editors use when they look at our stories.

The average news desk gets 400 items a day from PR firms and PR departments. One per cent gets used. This hasn't changed since 1924.

How can we make sure that *our* material belongs in that one per cent?

Note: People reading this PRCA guide may work in-house or in an agency. For the sake of brevity, I have used the word 'client' in this book to indicate the people we work for, whether that means an employer or, actually, a client.

GOOD MEDIA WRITING: THE BUSINESS CASE

William Zinsser, editor of *Life* and a media writing guru, said:

> *Executives at every level are prisoners of the notion that a simple style reflects a simple mind. The opposite is true: a simple story is the product of hard work and hard thinking.*
>
> *(Zinsser, 2006)*

There is a quotation attributed to Cicero, Martin Luther, Woodrow Wilson and Mark Twain along the following lines: 'I am sorry this letter is so long – I didn't have time to make it shorter'.

We know from our own experience that writing a terse, succinct account is much harder than putting the words down in a stream of consciousness. It takes a lot longer to write well.

So – is it worth it?

I think so. We are not writing for fun. We are trying to get stories about our clients' activities published by independent media with as little editing as possible. We want our clients' customers, staff, investors, neighbours (and other stakeholders) to read these stories and change their behaviour.

Editors have less time than ever. They delete most of what they are sent. Readers have less patience than ever. Even when they like a story, they typically only read half of it.

The point of our media writing is to plant *messages* in the minds of readers. That means our media material must first be *selected for inclusion*, then *survive the editorial process*, and then be *read – or consumed* – by people who like it, persist with it and ultimately change their ideas, opinions and actions as a result.

PR people are often accused of 'spray and pray'. The media don't like this. What they like is a story which is *intended for them* and which is written according to the *rules and conventions* that they learnt as trainees. Needless to say, the more powerful the media outlet, the more stringently its editors apply these rules.

If our media writing resembles our customers' own media writing, our success-rate will rocket.

Journalists and Editors – What Are They Like?

If you *were* a journalist or your sister works for *The Guardian*, you can skip this section. If not, it's useful to reflect on who our customers actually are and why they are different from the rest of us.

You may have noticed that journalists are a lot more like each other than any of them are like us. We work in teams; they never do. They are 'solo artistes' like singers or painters. They compete every day with people like themselves on other titles and with colleagues sitting at the next desk.

At some point early in their lives they have decided that they don't want to be part of politics, fashion, business, finance or sport ... instead, they want to be *outside* these areas of human activity, looking in and writing (or broadcasting) about what they observe. It's a strange way to make a living. It's also not much of a living; very few journalists make good money.

They are anxious. They always were, but more so with every month that passes. Journalists don't know if their title will exist in a year's time. They've all got friends who are now doing something else (which could be PR). As Andrew Marr says in '*My Trade*', it's a 'carnival of insecurity' (Marr, 2004).

There must be compensations. What are they? Expressing an independent point of view is one of them: 'speaking truth to power'. Simon Kelner put it nicely: 'I am a journalist, brought up to challenge authority, to contest the official version of events; to stand outside the establishment'.

Most journalists like to feel that they are champions of the public interest. They gravitate towards crusades or campaigns which expose wrongdoing and improve life for their readers and viewers. This is important for PR people like us; can we present our client's new initiative as something which will benefit millions? If so, we and the media will be on the same page.

Everyone working in the media is under pressure. Deadlines really are deadlines (unlike in most of the rest of the world).

Imagine being given a topic at the morning story conference; you are a general reporter, not a specialist, yet by mid-afternoon you must do your research and master the subject sufficiently to write a 600-word story which is authoritative, accurate, informative and interesting. Quite a challenge, but journalists do this day in, day out.

Lord Harmsworth (owner of *The Mail* and *Mirror*) once wittily said that journalism is a profession 'whose business is to explain to others what it does not personally understand'. Precisely. It takes a rare blend of abilities to be able to do this.

One of these characteristics is intense curiosity. You may have noticed how journalists often ask the same question three different ways in an interview. Clients can get annoyed, but the reporter is doing her job well – testing and probing to get at the real truth of the story.

Very few journalists are immune from the crushing effects of the twenty-first century media economy. Most are not doing what they dreamed of doing when they started out ... pounding the streets, knocking on doors, *finding* stories ... exclusives. Usually they do what we do – sit at a desk processing media material which streams in from people like us. Trade and technical titles are often staffed, these days, by an editor and one or two assistants. BBC regional news reporters used to travel with a crew of three or four; nowadays it's often just the presenter, on her own, operating her own camera and recording her own sound track.

No wonder the media revere Jeff Bezos, who bought *The Washington Post* in 2013 and employs 740 journalists.

How do the media feel about PR people? Sadly, they tend – in general – to disparage us. They depend on us for most of their material but they wish they didn't have to. They often blame PR for the economic plight of the media, which isn't really fair. All journalists know a few PR people they respect.

Why? It's usually because these PR people know what a story is and how to write it.

Learning to write media material which journalists admire – or at least respect – is, for most of us, the best way to our media customers' hearts.

THE ROI – MEDIA MESSAGES

PR works. That's why there are now 86,000 of us in the UK and why, according to the PRCA's 2018 census, the total UK PR budget is £13.8 billion.

Most people believe what they read in the media. Leaving aside un-branded, anonymous online 'news sources', we know that *real* media employ professionals to find stories, research them, verify them and present them to us in a manner we find useful and credible. We have IPSO to regulate our media; most journalists would sooner die than write anything untrue, but there are occasional exceptions, and even the best reporters sometimes can't read their notes.

There are cynics, like Roman Abramovich: 'A hamster is just a rat with good PR'.

There are true believers, like Michael Wolff: 'The media are a more influential force in our lives and in the world's changing beliefs than politics or governments ever were'.

There are normal people like my grandmother: 'There it is in black and white!'

Most of us, most of the time, believe what we read in most media. Hence the 'power of PR'.

I suggest it makes sense to be very careful about the *media messages* which our stories convey. This is because, knowing the immense influence which the media exert, we should treat opportunities for coverage like gold dust.

Sheer coverage is a bit like advertising. It can create 'awareness', which is a useful start, but it can do so much more. Awareness ('I know that brand') is the start of a process known as the *hierarchy of effects*, but it's only the start. When David Ogilvy, the Scotsman who more-or-less re-engineered the US advertising industry, wrote his copywriting rules he insisted that copywriters should arouse interest, provide information, trigger an emotional reaction and provide a 'call to action'.

You can see the result when you visit the dentist and leaf through 40-year-old copies *of National Geographic* or *Reader's Digest.* The ads set out to take the reader on a journey all the way up to trial purchase.

This rarely happens in the twenty-first century. Ads aim to create awareness, but that's it. The rest of the work is nowadays the province of PR.

I hope this makes sense to you, because it's where advertising and PR are like brothers and sisters rather than spitting cousins. The point of our work as media writers is (usually) to sell something, to change people's feelings about our client's planning application from hostile to neutral or positive, to get lines down the street outside the new restaurant on opening night ... and so on; a business objective usually expressed in pounds, dollars or euros.

This is where carefully thought-out media messages make all the difference.

Most of us forget information fairly quickly unless it has a direct bearing on our personal lives. When we consume media our retention is even more fleeting – there is just so much of it. Knowing this about our ultimate audiences, how can we take steps to make sure, as far as possible, that they remember *something* about our client after they've read our coverage and moved on?

The best answer, I suggest, is to be careful, creative and ruthless when we are developing the media messages that our PR work is meant to convey. This is difficult. Here again, we are tackling exactly the same kind of challenge that confronts our colleagues in advertising creative departments.

If we ask a typical client or employer for the 'key messages' for this year or this quarter, we will usually receive a list of 20 or 30 vitally important statements about features and benefits. The list has been compiled by an email committee. It's no use: what we need are *three*. If we are very accomplished and diligent, *one* of these messages may stick.

Does this sound pessimistic? Try a simple test in the pub. Ask a friend to come up with *three* things they know about a famous brand – IBM, BMW, Chanel, Easyjet ... they've got to answer quickly – we are looking for 'top of mind' recall. Most people can do this. Then ask your friend to come up with a *fourth*. Most people are stumped. (You can win drinks with this game.)

What this proves is that getting people to remember *anything at all* about a brand is an achievement. Knowing this, it makes sense for us to concentrate our efforts on projecting a *small* number of messages in any given campaign or programme period.

Political communicators in Washington say that the art of engagement means telling people your message, then telling them again, then again, then again, then again, then again ... at the point where you yourself are bored to death, the message will just be starting to get traction.

Michael Dell has a brain like a computer but he knows that most people don't. His instructions to us at GCI were clear: 'there will be three media messages this quarter per campaign. After three months we will see if they are working. If so, continue, If not, review'.

Here are some guidelines which may be useful in deciding on media messages:

Distinctive	*apparently* original, unusual, different
Simple	short, everyday words – no jargon
Few	three is ideal (we remember things in triplets)
Relevant	why does this matter to me?
Consistent	consistency aids memorability
Attractive	pleasing, warm, human ... the charm factor

We often find, especially in FMCG, that our messages have already been determined by the client's advertising agency – who frequently get briefed first. This may be helpful but sometimes not – some advertising messages translate into PR but some don't. When we need to develop our own from scratch, a useful approach is Brand Character Analysis. A BCA system is described in the Appendix.

THE MEDIA WRITING CHALLENGE: EDITORIAL CHOICE

In 1924, Basil Clarke, founder of Britain's first PR agency, said: 'Only one item in a hundred submitted to the newspapers has any chance of being published'.

Nearly 100 years later Anthony Hilton, doyen of city editors, said: 'The trick is to spot the one press release in a hundred that is worth reading'.

This 'one-per cent rule' may be a law of nature, but it's getting worse. The more PR people there are the more competition there is for editorial attention. The fewer outlets there are the more intense the competition becomes for space and time.

Editing is a two-stage process. First, an item has to be selected for possible inclusion; as a 'possible', it has to survive against all the other stories competing for a particular slot or segment. Next, it has to be cut or adapted to fit the amount of space or time available. Outlets always have more material available than they can use. That's why good stories often disappear into the void, even when writers have spent hours or days putting them together.

There are many reasons why stories are spiked, binned or deleted. Some are late or old, meaning they are no longer *news*. It's surprising how often this happens. Journalists frequently receive media material which has no relevance to the topics they cover: 'spray and pray' strikes again. The media hate this because it is a complete waste of time. They frequently receive press releases which are evidently of great interest to the company sending them but of no earthly interest to anyone else. This unhelpful experience hints at an agency which has promised their client they will issue *four releases a month*, regardless of whether or not there is anything worth saying.

But over and above these sins is the basic fact that the media receive far more stories from people like us than they can possibly use. The volume is so great that it's not uncommon for journalists to pick the first four stories they like from that day's 400, choose a further four as back-up and delete the rest. It pays dividends to call and place a story before we send it. Yes, this takes longer – but it ensures that our editorial customers are waiting for our story rather than never seeing it at all. There is a section on placing or 'selling-in' stories later in this book.

Clients sometimes confuse PR with advertising. When Jonathan Guthrie was first writing Lex in the *Financial Times* (*FT*) he received a 'press release' from the managing director of a quoted company. He thought the story was interesting so he turned it into a short item. The next day he heard from the MD: 'Thank you for printing our news – but, next time, please don't change the words'.

This is a comic example, but clients very often misunderstand how the process works, especially when they are new to PR. It's a good idea to brief them thoroughly on the extreme level of competition for media attention and the skills PR people use to win clients 'more than their fair share'. This is sometimes called *managing expectations*. The PRCA offers a workshop for clients which shows them, among other things, how to work hand-in-glove with their PR advisors; what the media expect from them and how to help their agency produce material that the media want to use.

This idea of clients' 'fair share of attention' is worth exploring. If we are lucky enough to work for Virgin, Greenpeace or Mick Jagger, the media automatically assume that whatever they are doing or saying will be worth reporting. You could say that it's easy to get coverage for clients like this; they know it, so what they expect from their PR people isn't usually volume.

But most of us don't: we work for organisations or brands who need to work hard to get their voice heard above the clamour. What *is* their 'fair share of attention'? It's worth calculating; what most clients pay us for is to win them a *quantity* and *quality* of media coverage which would not otherwise come their way. It's subjective: some clients believe (wrongly) that *whatever* they are doing ought to attract media attention; others believe (wrongly) that *nothing* they do is interesting to the media.

The best way to overcome the media writing challenge (apart from writing well) is to invest time in getting to know our media customers personally. Journalists like it if they believe we are genuinely trying to provide them with a good service. They respond positively. This means we have to know a lot about them ... what they have been writing, the angle they usually take, whether they prefer interviews face to face or over the phone, whether they insist on an exclusive or are happy with an exclusive angle … when they like to be called … there is a lot to know. They are all different.

But this is *media relations*, the subject of another PRCA Practice Guide.

Some journalists are very demanding. But most aren't. Here is Barry Fox, a technology writer who has seen it all: 'We don't expect PR people to have all the answers. We *do* expect them to know who does have the answers, get them and not garble the reply'. He is not asking much. But the fact he said it suggests this basic level of service to our media customers is not as common as it should be.

'Apart from writing well'. We are probably not doing PR for Elon Musk. Our client has *real news* once in a blue moon. They have some interesting opinions. They conduct research which sometimes raises eyebrows. They are a successful organisation with strong leadership. They know where they are going and they have a plan. They are good employers and good neighbours. They are ambitious; they sense the value of a high media profile and they are paying us to achieve it for them. But they are not Elon Musk.

What will make the difference?

Good media writing.

B2B AND B2C – WHAT'S THE DIFFERENCE?

As PR evolves we get more specialised. It's what our clients want and it's what most of us want, too. More to the point, it's what our media customers want.

There are major specialisations like health care (itself sub-divided into Rx and OTC), financial communications, government communications, technology (with at least five sub-divisions) … and then there is the general distinction between business-to-business (B2B) and business-to-consumer (B2C).

Most PR people tend to think of themselves, or become, more expert in one or the other as their careers progress.

When it comes to media writing, there is a school of thought which says that B2B and B2C demand very different styles of composition. B2B should be factual, dry and even dull. B2C should be bright, vivid and entertaining.

I suggest that the distinction doesn't really exist. Or at least shouldn't.

It's true that people using B2B outlets are doing so purposefully. They seek useful information, probably as part of their work. As a rule of thumb, people consuming B2C media are pursuing amusement, edification, entertainment and interesting information, sometimes with an aim in mind and sometimes as a diversion, but always for personal rather than professional reasons.

But they are all still people. They respond to drama, surprise, shock, humour and novelty in exactly the same way.

I was taught that all media stories – whatever their apparent subject – are *in fact* human-interest stories. We are interested in a new enterprise productivity tool because (if we are a CIO) we may need to consider installing it; but even the most dedicated CIO will be much more interested in who developed it, the challenges they overcame on the way, the team who burnt the midnight oil meeting their deadline; he or she will be very interested in the people who are meant to use it and the difference it will make to their working lives.

If we approach B2B stories from this *human-interest* angle they are likely to be much more readable and therefore much more effective.

The same goes for B2B photography and video. The new aero engine is probably a thing of beauty, but our attention will be far more closely gripped if we can see human beings working on it. All of us are naturally fascinated by other people. Rolls-Royce, as it happens, is particularly good at this.

We will return to the idea of human interest later in the book. It is probably journalists' most important composition rule.

For now, let me leave the idea with you that there is no real difference between B2B and B2C media writing, except in the fine details of content and style.

HOW JOURNALISTS WRITE

Journalists call what they write *stories*. This means that everything – a news item, a news feature, a review, a survey, a case study – has a beginning, middle and end. The rules for story structure are well established and fairly rigid. There's a reason: people like *stories* (not statements) and journalists have to make sure people *want* to read what they have taken so much trouble to produce.

Stories are intrinsically interesting. Most of our conversation consists of stories. Media stories can be informative, uplifting, shocking, amusing, entertaining, disturbing ... they must always be engaging. They must have a rhythm, a pace and a shape which readers can recognise and feel comfortable with.

The same rules apply to us.

The 'art' of journalism is writing simply, in words that everyone can understand. This sounds easy but it isn't. *The Mirror* used to brag that it employed more Oxbridge graduates than *The Telegraph*. Using simple language demands greater technical ability.

Media writing is getting harder. This is because people have less and less patience. If they encounter difficult or incomprehensible language they switch off, click away, scroll down or turn the page at once. All readers have their own threshold: scientists are happy with technical terms that a business audience won't tolerate. It's important to think about the reader before we put finger to keyboard; this can mean writing the same story in two or three different versions.

David Randall's 'top tip' in *The Universal Journalist* is: 'Take command of the material'. He means we should spend time researching, absorbing, browsing the subject before we start writing. Ideally we (and journalists) should leave a few hours between 'taking command' and starting to write, but neither we nor they have the opportunity to do this very often. If we can, though, something magic happens: while we are *not* thinking about our story it will take shape in our minds.

Readers are busy. There are thousands of calls on their attention every day. Most of us tend to skim content, only stopping when we feel sure that an item deserves our time. The media's solution is, of course, an arresting headline. These are not usually written by journalists but by editors or subs (on titles which still employ members of this dwindling species). Headlines are *hooks*.

Pictures can also be hooks. Whether words or images they are saying: 'Read this! It's worth it'.

The *lead* (sometimes spelt '*lede*') or *intro* is all important. Journalists work hard on their leads. They don't want someone else re-writing them. The lead is meant to encapsulate the story according to a formula which we will talk about later in the book: who? what? when? where? why? how? how much? The litmus test on re-reading a draft lead is: so what?

If the lead fails this test, all the journalists' work has been in vain.

Media writing is completely different from the kind of writing which is admired at school, college or in the corporate world. Trainee journalists have to be 're-calibrated'. No more multi-syllable words! No more 30-word sentences! No more 20-line paragraphs!

Words should be short (three syllables maximum); they don't have to be 'Anglo-Saxon' but they often are. Sentences should be 12 words or less. A paragraph is three sentences. All this makes media stories easy to read and take in. We probably don't notice how clipped journalists' style is when we are reading our favourite media brands because we are so used to it.

For people who have been educated in *academic* English it can be difficult switching to this different way of using words and constructing copy. An editor receiving our media material can tell at a glance if we know how to write like a journalist, so it's a skill worth developing.

The journalist sits down to start his or her draft. What's the main thought in their mind? It won't be 'human interest' because for a journalist that's second nature. It's the *lead*: how to put as much of the 'punch' of the item as possible at the top of the story. Journalists know that once they've nailed the lead the rest of the piece will flow naturally: development, quotes, references, context, consequences and elaboration.

Most journalists will also be thinking about *exclusivity*. This doesn't necessarily mean that they are the only writer to be given the story (though that puts a smile on any journalist's face) but it *does* mean approaching the story from their own point of view ... finding a way to present the facts in a way that seems original and different from other journalists' coverage of the same topic.

Quotations (or quotes) are important. The rule of thumb is that a story should be half quotes, either direct (in quotation marks) or in indirect speech. This is the best way to make the story 'live' and to ensure that its human interest is front and central. Journalists dread being given quotes which are, in the parlance, 'corporate happy-speak'. They much prefer to interview spokespeople and get their own quotes, but sometimes neither time nor corporate rules make this possible. We will talk about *good quotes* later in the book.

Journalists do their best to keep the story short. If their title has subs this is less important – a sub's main responsibility is to cut – but these days, subs are in short supply, so most journalists try to write to length. This is even more important in broadcasting, where every second counts.

A golden rule in media writing is 'brevity equals quality'. For us, this means that a press release should contain all the key facts and not much else. Journalists often complain about receiving over-blown media material from PR sources. If they want the story they then have to spend time cutting it or even re-writing it, often with gritted teeth: aren't PR people supposed to *save them time*?

Verification: if a journalist is writing for a major title there will be specialists whose role is to authenticate facts, figures and quotes before the item is published. On smaller outlets the journalist has to do his or her best to verify everything while they are composing the piece. This is an area where PR people can save journalists a lot of time by providing references and sources.

When journalists are dealing with PR material their verification antennae are on full alert. There is no such thing as a credulous journalist. If they are not naturally suspicious they are trained to be. My editor said: 'I don't want the story they give you. I don't even want the story behind that. I want the story behind *that*!' This is worth bearing in mind when we are composing media material. Unless the writer knows and trusts us, they will be sceptical. We can make their lives easier (and earn their trust) by making no statements or claims which cannot be independently verified.

On larger media brands it will be someone else's job to edit the journalist's draft, but very often – especially at trade, technical and professional outlets – they have to do it themselves. We will talk about 'self-editing' later in the book.

The 'golden rule' here is to leave a pause – an hour or so, ideally – then look at the draft with fresh eyes. It's a very bad idea to send something out straight from the keyboard – though sometimes, of course, neither we nor journalists have any choice. Another 'golden rule' is that *everything can be improved* – shorter, sharper, clearer, simpler, easier to read.

Most journalists look at PR material with a jaundiced eye. When we meet them for a drink we can expect a barrage of complaints: 'You PR people … you don't know how to write a story! You don't seem to know what we need! Most of you don't know how the media work!' And so on. Our job is to stand out from the crowd on behalf of our clients or employers. This means looking at stories from a journalist's point of view and writing them in much the same way. If we can do this it makes a real difference to our hit rate, our clients' satisfaction and our own reputation.

THE JOURNALIST'S PR CHALLENGE

You are a busy editor or writer and you receive this on your screen:

> *I am very pleased to welcome Stephen to our growing team. His extensive knowledge of the area and range of experience in dealing with high-net-worth individuals will be a significant asset to our team. His appointment not only enhances our presence in the area but also emphasises our commitment to our clients there.*

Notice the redundant words … extensive … significant … enhances … commitment.

There is something leaden, dead, dull about it. But it's an important story…

This is part of a genuine press release from a major bank. It would break your heart to use it as it stands, so you need to make at least one phone call and then re-write it.

The PR person responsible has *not* saved his or her media customer time.

> *ABC offers the complete package. A life-proof design with smart technology. Whether you're chilling pool-side or stuck burning the midnight oil in the office, this phone is built to keep up and provide users with peace of mind.*

What on earth is this? A press release? No – it's obviously a piece of advertising copy cut-and-pasted into a 'press release'. But it comes from a world leader in mobile communications.

You are a busy editor. You *must* carry this story, but you would sooner die than publish it as it stands. Here again, you need to spend time calling the company, finding out the facts about the new 'ABC' and writing the news item properly. Once again, the PR person who emitted this nonsense has *not* provided his or her media contacts with a service.

We could fill the book with examples like this, picked at random from the online press rooms of brand leaders who should know better. And they *do* know better, so what's going on?

Very likely, these PR people are writing copy for their clients or employers – not for their customers.

It's a cardinal error. The media complain about it all the time.

Journalists' PR challenge is only too often wading through piles of guff – poorly conceived, carelessly written, presented by people who neither know nor care about what the media need – in pursuit of real stories which can be published.

If we make this easier for them by sending material which they *don't* have to research and re-write, we will quickly become 'media favourites'.

JOURNALISTS' RULES

Journalism is regarded as a profession in the UK. The qualifications awarded by the National Council for the Training of Journalists are based on rigorous exams and have long been seen as the global gold standard.

Journalists (or reporters) were traditionally hired as 'cubs' and trained for years in a kind of apprenticeship scheme while studying for the National Qualification in Journalism (NQJ). The journalists we meet today are equally likely to have completed a course at their own expense before finding work.

Either way, journalists in this country take their role seriously and place a lot of importance on knowing how to perform it well. They have high standards and – here's the point – appreciate it when PR people demonstrate that they share the same professional criteria. Good media writing is the key requirement for them – and us.

Journalists are taught to approach a story with the reader in mind. My editor called this the 'mum on bus' test. We had to imagine mum on the top deck of a bus, reading our story. She can't resist turning to her neighbour and saying: 'Oooh – do you know what I've just read in the paper?'

This sets the bar quite high, but it's a good basic discipline. If we *don't* think readers are going to be gripped by what we've written, why are we bothering?

This rule can be resolved to a set of guidelines:

Make it Interesting.

Our reader (viewer, listener, browser) has to think: 'Wow – really?' before they decide to spend any time at all with our story.

This means our headline and intro must be instantly compelling. Major media outlets employ subs who are experts at this, but if you work in PR you have to do it yourself.

Make it Relevant.

Our reader has to think: 'This is important to me'. Easy enough if our story is aimed at a specialist B2B target or a niche B2C market, but capturing the attention of browsers or a general interest audience presents us with more of a challenge.

Make it Meaningful.

'I need to change something'. An opinion, a sentiment, a behaviour. If nothing happens after people have read our story we have failed. Advertisers describe this as a 'call to action'.

Make it Enjoyable.

'I like this story'. Even the most factual B2B item should be a pleasure to read. Attention spans are shrinking, no-one has much patience, it is only too easy to scroll down or click away (or turn the page). Enjoyment is the glue that will, if we are lucky, keep readers engaged right to the end.

Make it Simple.

Not a word wasted. The simplest way to present media material is a list. This isn't writing, but the popularity of lists illustrates the golden rule that simplicity is king.

Warmth, Humanity, Charm.

We all have our favourite journalists and writers. What makes them stand out? It's probably because we feel they are talking *directly* to us, one human being to another, and they write like an entertaining story-teller in the pub. Some people are born with this talent. For the rest of us, the best way to acquire it is to read a lot of material by writers we like, and hope that some of their technique will magically transfer itself to us. Which it does.

We've got three releases to write today, in between taking client calls and attending meetings. How realistic is it to expect all three to be gems which deserve a place in our scrapbook? Not very. When you work in PR, over-load is frequently the enemy of quality and can even cause despair. The point is to do the *best we can*, in the time available, to make as much of our writing first-class as possible.

RESEARCHING A STORY

David Randall's *The Universal Journalist* is a bible of good media writing practice. He says: 'Take command of the material'. Graham Wallas in *The Art of Thought* cites *preparation* as the starting point for any creative process. Other experts talk about 'immersion'.

It's probably obvious, but still worth saying: the more time we can spend researching and exploring the subject, the better our written material is likely to be.

Time is the problem: it's in short supply. Even so, it pays to set aside half an hour to 'take command of the material' ... what have other media writers been saying about the topic? Is there a historical background which casts an interesting light on the subject? Are there wider issues affecting the news we are describing? What else are people doing in this field? Have there been academic papers or speeches which we can use to illuminate our story? Are there links to other times, other places or other industries which we can use to set our story in a more interesting context?

When Graham Wallas was writing this meant a trip to the library. For us it's easy; we all know how to browse. It is time well spent: our aim is to make our story the *one in a hundred* which the media will like enough to publish. What our client gives us may be vanilla; we can, with a bit of luck, turn it into media gold by researching around and behind the basic facts.

If we have time, an even better way to get to the heart of a client's story is to talk to customers. If you have had the opportunity to do this, you will know how valuable it is: half an hour's listening (usually while tagging along on sales calls) suddenly reveals a whole new way to frame and compose our story. We *know* it will pass the 'mum on bus' test.

Next, we need to give our brains a bit of time to work on the material we have explored. Experts on creativity tell us that the best ideas emerge when we are *not* concentrating on the subject. Have you noticed how often a great PR idea comes to mind when you are cooking, walking the dog or playing World of Warcraft?

What this suggests is that we should always allow a chunk of time – an hour or more – between 'taking command of the material' and putting our fingers to the keyboard.

INTERVIEW TIPS

We often need to interview a client executive to get the information for a story. Even if we don't have to, it's the best way to acquire the facts we want – much better than an emailed brief.

Clients are frequently nervous about the media. This makes sense, in a way: from their point of view, the downside of a media story that *goes wrong* far outweighs the upside of good media coverage.

It helps to manage client interviews in a way which allays any possible nervousness and encourages them to speak freely. The more we can make the 'interview' feel like a conversation between friends, the more likely we are to hear what is *really* exciting our client about the product or service we are describing.

Here are some tips which may help to streamline the process:

When you set up the interview, don't call it an 'interview'. It can be a short meeting, a discussion or a briefing instead. This solves the problem of anxiety about an 'interview' and by-passes the client's possible nervousness about the media.

Schedule the meeting, if you can, at a time of day when they are not pre-occupied with other work. This usually means at the end of the day. Our aim is to get them to relax and speak freely.

Ask for 40 minutes. You want them to tell you about their personal role and their feelings – why they are excited, motivated, what they did, what it means to them – so it pays to allow time to let them move on from 'corporate-speak' and talk person-to-person, just as they would if they were speaking to a friend in a bar.

Homework: find out as much as you possibly can in advance. Good reporters do this. The point is to win the interviewee's confidence, and perhaps respect, by making it obvious that you have earned the right to take up their time. Everyone reacts positively to a well-informed interviewer.

Ask if you can record the conversation. This will help you get your quotes right and also enables you to look at the interviewee during the conversation. At the same time, make written notes: interviewees feel, correctly, that this lends importance to the dialogue.

Be a 'good listener'. This means showing interest, fascination, surprise. Encourage your interviewee to speak openly and with enthusiasm; your own enthusiasm will make this happen.

Invite them to look over your draft to 'fact-check'. This opens up the possibility that they will try to avert risk by copying the draft to all and sundry – but not if you give them the draft in hard copy.

Explain your deadline. Give them a 24x7 contact number. Try to avoid email, which encourages 'what do you think?' copying and a committee result. Instead, encourage them to call you and talk through any points which they are not sure about. Similarly, make sure you have their mobile number in case you need to clarify facts while you are writing your draft.

Try to capture their personal style of speaking. This makes a piece of editorial *come alive* like nothing else can. A good example is James Hurley's interview with Paul Eagland of BDO in *The Times* of 26 January 2018.

Remember that a good editorial item consists of 50 per cent reported speech, either between inverted commas – direct quotes – or indirect: 'At this point Annabel said she doubted that the market for garden humidifiers would take off as quickly as predicted'.

You can combine the two: 'At this point Annabel said she doubted that the market for garden humidifiers would take off as quickly as predicted. "It would be nice to think that most urban gardens will be humidified by 2020", she said. "But I can't see it happening" '.

Try to paint a verbal picture of the interviewee and the setting. Introduce drama (literally 'action') into the narrative so that your readers can imagine themselves being there with you: 'Annabel stood up and moved to the window. She seemed to be studying the weather – cloudy, grey, cold. Turning back, she said: "..."'.

When you write the interview, especially if it is with a client executive, keep the tone level. Beware of writing the story 'up'. Awe and admiration may pass muster in a captive outlet but they don't go down well with independent media editors. Likewise, moderate your interviewee's language if it is full of 'world's leading' style corporate exaggeration.

Finally, the small courtesies. A note to thank the interviewee for his or her time (even though you are both being paid for this work). Thanks again for looking over the draft; thirdly, send a copy of the interview when it is published, thanking them for their time and trouble.

The same approach works well for an op-ed (600–1,000 words to be published over the interviewee's by-line). Some clients like to write their own op-eds, in which case our function is to tidy it up; but most don't. We need to interview them and then present them with a draft. Needless to say, it will be written in the first person – more like an essay than most other forms of media writing. Here again, it helps bring the piece to life if we can catch the verbal style of the 'author'.

COMPOSITION

Headlines and Leads

> *The most important sentence in any article is the first one. If it doesn't induce the reader to proceed to the second sentence, your article is dead.*
>
> *William Zinsser,* On Writing Well
> *(Zinsser, 2006)*

The average reader's attention span is around 10 seconds. Whether they are turning pages or scrolling, they won't persist with media material unless it grabs their interest immediately.

The first gateway for a media writer is the headline. If you are a journalist, somebody else looks after the headlines – a specialist sub. But if you're us, you need to master the art of the 'hooky' headline.

The second gateway is the lead. It has to make them want to continue reading for more than 10 seconds. How?

Headlines Must Raise Eyebrows and Dilate Pupils

In a speech it's called a 'grabber'. It makes people sit up and pay attention.

Headlines arouse shock, surprise, outrage, curiosity and sometimes amusement. All are emotional reactions. A response that says: 'How could that be?' or 'Surely not!' One of the best ways is to frame our headline as a question, which automatically provokes curiosity. Questions (like lists) are drearily familiar from click-bait, but they still work when used intelligently in real editorial.

Imagine we are running a campaign to reduce obesity. We have a new research paper from Professor Smith which studies the role of hunger management in lowering calorie intake. There are numerous ways we can write the headline to intrigue and 'hook' our readers:

> *Diets pointless unless hunger controlled, says Professor*
>
> *20 million Brits can't keep their hands off cakes, says new research*
>
> *How long does it take to lose 20 kg? Forever, says Professor*
>
> *Why people eat too much: university study exposes the truth*

Average couch potato weighs more than couch, says Professor Smith

Rampant hunger costs Britain 200,000 working days a year, says Professor

Controlling hunger could save 15,000 lives a year – Professor Smith

Leads Must Convince Readers to Invest Their Time

The classic media lead answers the questions: 'who, what, when, where, why, how ... how much?'

There are other ways to draw the reader in. We can tell a story, intrigue them with surprising facts or statistics, quote a fascinating statement from an authority, overturn conventional beliefs, tell a success story, describe a human problem, paint a verbal picture...

Readers have to think: 'Hmm. This could be interesting. I'll read on'.

Professor Smith of Felixstowe University has discovered that ***diets don't work*** *unless people receive training and support in managing their appetites. 'It's all about controlling hunger', he says. This surprising result comes from a three-year study of 640 people diagnosed as clinically obese.*

Professor Smith was working late in his laboratory at Felixstowe University. He was analysing the results of a three-year study of 640 overweight people on diets. He couldn't believe his eyes: 'It suddenly stood out, clear as daylight, that diets are useless unless people learn to control their appetites', he says. 'We always thought the key factor was calorie intake, but it's not. What matters is managing hunger'.

Over 20 million people on diets will achieve ***no weight reduction whatsoever*** *unless they learn to manage their appetites. This is the shock finding from new research at Felixstowe University, where 640 people with obesity have been studied for three years by Professor Smith. 'We have been wrong for years', he says. 'It's not about calorie intake. It's about learning how to control hunger'.*

Why do millions of people on diets fail to lose weight? This question led Professor Smith of Felixstowe University to set up a three-year study of 640 people with severe weight problems. What he found was astonishing: 'It's got nothing to do with calorie management, as we always thought', he says. 'It's all about hunger control – something entirely different'.

The weight-loss industry has a new elephant in the room. If you thought getting slimmer was a matter of cutting down the calories, think again. 'It's not about calorie intake, as we always believed', says Professor Smith, who led a three-year research study at Felixstowe University. 'It's about managing hunger successfully. Dieters need entirely different kinds of advice and support'.

Jessica Jones, a 36-year-old mother of three from Lowestoft, had been dieting for years in an effort to lose a few pounds. 'Nothing worked', she says. 'I tried everything but I just couldn't shift it. I was getting desperate'. Then she enrolled in a weight-loss study led by Professor Smith of Felixstowe University. Within six months Ms Jones was ten pounds slimmer. The answer to her prayer was a key discovery from

> *Professor Smith's study: 'calorie intake was a blind alley for Jessica and millions of others', he says. 'What matters is hunger management – learning how to control your appetite'.*

There are countless ways to draft a successful headline and lead. Most journalists try to imagine their typical reader. What will make him or her pause long enough to read the headline and be interested enough to want to read the lead? What's in it for the reader? Subs often throw copy back at reporters with the question 'So what?' We should ask ourselves the same question before we start writing our stories.

Format and Structure

Most of the material we offer our media customers should follow similar rules of format and structure, whether it's a release, a media advisory, a news feature, a feature, an op-ed, a case study, a background briefing, an interview, a profile, a review....

Material we are posting directly online should use the same rules of structure but – obviously – doesn't need the formatting top-and-tail described here.

Dateline

It's good practice to state where the story comes from as well as when it was issued. For example: Manchester, 12 June 2019.

If our client is based in London but the story has been released at, for example, the Mobile World Congress, the dateline should make that clear: Barcelona (date).

Embargo or 'For Immediate Release'

Embargoes are used less and less in the age of a 24 × 7 × 52 global news cycle, online and MSM, because it is increasingly likely that media outlets will choose to break them. If you are giving a story to journalists you know and trust, the embargo system can still work. If you are sending a release out to a general list, the embargo statement is more-or-less pointless: don't rely on it.

I have heard editors laughing at the presence of an embargo at the head of a news release.

By the same token, if you are not using an embargo it looks odd to say 'For Immediate Release'. This can also cause mirth in the newsroom.

Headline

Ideally, no more than one line. Will the headline appear in your subject-box? If not, why not?

Dek or Sub-headline

Common in the US. Best avoided in UK and European media material.

Lead (Sometimes 'lede')

The intro para or 'top of the story'. Who, what, when, where, why, how ... how much?

Narrative Intro Hook

This is how Alex Lawson began a story about problems at GSK in the Indie:

> *The first thing many drivers see when taking the M4 into London is GlaxoSmithKline's towering offices greeting those coming from Heathrow, arriving in Britain to the sight of its largest drug maker.*

The *second* paragraph gives the facts which we would normally expect to find in the first:

> *But a thick cloud of scandal has recently come to enshroud Britain's biggest pharmaceuticals firm as the Serious Fraud Office looks into the company's dealings.*

This can be a very effective, different, way of capturing the reader's interest.

Body Copy

Development, implications, proof points, quotes. The ideal news story consists of 50 per cent quotes – either reported speech or verbatim inside inverted commas.

Quotes

Human, vivid – they should sound like a real human being speaking to another human being. Avoid at all costs 'corporate happy-speak', hype and clichés.

Theme

One theme per item. We can sometimes inadvertently meander from one theme to another, and even three or four, when drafting an item for release. We should spot this at the self-editing stage, otherwise the media will have to chop our material up into its constituent themes.

Cross-heads or Sub-heads

Mainly used as a typographical device to avoid the 'wall of copy' and make our material easier to read. Also has the virtue of making our item resemble conventional media writing.

Pictures, Illustrations, Graphics, Infographics

Ideally not embedded but available from a separate source.

Captions

Factual. It is best to leave witty captions to *The Economist.*

Clips

Available separately. Always worth offering if possible; most major news brands think online first, where clips and animations significantly increase PR story take up.

References

It is good practice to give references to sources of facts and figures quoted in our copy – it saves work for the reporters and fact checkers. If few, links in the text. If numerous, a list of links at the end.

Notes to Editors

Five lines in italics. If more is needed (for instance, if we are sending our material to outlets who are unlikely to know anything about our client) it is helpful to offer 'Fast Facts' separately.

Enquiries

Journalists like an immediate answer to their queries (deadlines) and are often not working during normal office hours.

It makes sense to provide at least two enquiry points, and ideally four. If the client is happy to answer media enquiries, and has been media trained, we can offer two contacts at the agency and two at the client.

Short Form and Long Form

What's the difference? When it comes to composition, not as much as we might expect.

Short form (releases, briefing papers, letters to the editor and so on) and long form (features, news features, op-eds, case studies) both have to perform the same function: capture the reader's attention, persuade them to start reading the piece and then read enough of it to make a difference to their opinions, sentiments and behaviour.

Brevity is the key. It may sound odd to speak of 'brevity' in relation to long-form items of 1,200 words, but the point is to make our *expression* short, sharp and clear regardless of the overall length of the piece.

The cards are stacked against us. The Poynter Institute carried out an eye-tracking study of 582 people consuming news material, measuring 102,000 eye stops. They found that stories over 11 paragraphs long typically lose readers half-way through.

With long-form material we have permission to use more colour, adjectives and adverbs. We can offer more verbal illustrations and provide lengthier narratives. But everything else is the same: we need a gripping lead, we must keep our sentences and paragraphs short and we must use quotes and descriptions of human activity to engage and retain readers' interest – even when the story appears to be about valves, logistics parks or derivatives.

The Human Factor and Illustrations

What interests human beings isn't facts, figures, statements and objects – it's other people. We are designed to pay close attention to people and make rapid judgements about them. We are fascinated by other humans and most of us have exceptionally good recall when it comes to how other people looked and what we thought of them.

Tests show that the memorability of speeches is mainly due to how the speaker looked, spoke and behaved: what he or she *said* accounts for only a small fraction of the impact.

With this in mind it makes sense to frame our media stories around *people* to the greatest possible extent. This is probably second nature when we are composing a B2C item but may be less obvious when we are dealing with a B2B or corporate topic. But the same rules apply.

When Rolls-Royce opened a plant extension in Derby they multiplied their coverage by offering photography showing engineers, spookily back-lit, next to the giant silhouette of an aero-engine. The picture grabbed readers' (and editors') interest because it made the story about *people* working at the plant – whereas the engines, the budget and the economic consequences, though relevant, would not have made for such a compelling news item.

F-secure, a digital security specialist, turned a technical story into something everyone wanted to read. F-secure put together 'lash-up' Wi-Fi hotspots and positioned them in key London locations. Passers-by saw a strong signal on their mobile devices and clicked on the hotspots, scrolling through the terms and conditions, clicking on 'Agree' and then sitting down nearby to use the service. Hidden in the terms and conditions was F-Secure's 'Herod Clause'; users had unwittingly agreed to sacrifice their first-born child. What won this clever idea global pick-up was the pictures which accompanied the story: people using the service, unaware of what they had agreed to, sitting happily on walls in the City and Westminster, glued to their devices. These images conveyed F-secure's marketing message dramatically.

Reporters are trained to look for the human angle in any story they are covering. We can maximise our clients' coverage by doing exactly the same thing. We should recommend accompanying pictures, clips and infographics every time: they are a small investment for a potentially enormous ROI. Here's a litmus test: if a story *doesn't* deserve an illustration, is it really a story that anyone is going to want to read?

Media pictures should be taken by specialist media photographers. They know what picture editors want. Brochure shots won't do. Picture editors have a lot of choice: Fiona Shields, *The Guardian*'s head of photography, says that her team receives 30,000 images every 24 hours (*The Guardian*, 2018).

Media Language

Good media writing is entirely different from the kind of writing which gets good marks at school, college and in the corporate world. Here, long words and complex sentences usually impress our teachers, professors and clients.

In media writing it's the exact opposite. What works are short words, short sentences and short paragraphs. Some people say that the corporate world would do well to take a leaf out of the media's book. Winston Churchill is supposed to have insisted, when wartime Prime Minister, that he would not look at any proposal more than a single page in length.

Vocabulary: Three syllables at most, ideally one or two. This doesn't necessarily mean 'Anglo-Saxon', though it often does. Avoid latinate, multisyllabic constructions, which are often jargon or technical terms, if you possibly can. This is harder than it sounds.

It used to be said (by *The Mirror*) that *The Mirror* employed more Oxbridge graduates than *The Telegraph*. It takes more skill to write about complicated subjects in simple language.

Sentences: Twelve words at most. But make each sentence a proper sentence, with a subject, verb and object. Unless you are writing a novel. This is also much harder than it sounds and takes practice.

Paragraphs: Three sentences at most. For people used to corporate writing, this seems strange. But look at the average paragraph length in your preferred news outlet. The aim is to make every story, whether it is itself straightforward or intricate, easy for readers to follow and absorb.

What matters is the *read-through-rate*. If our target audiences read our material to the end, there is a good chance they will change their opinions and maybe their behaviour. If not, probably not.

Enemies of Clarity

The media's writing challenge is, in some ways, easier than ours. They have to please the subs (if there are any) and the editor. We have to satisfy our *clients* before the media ever get to see what we have written.

This can be tricky. Clients are not usually natural-born writers – they are normally paid for other skills. As a result, they often express themselves in language which does not convert well into compelling media material. These are some of the main problems:

Industrial tribalism: The second level of Maslow's Hierarchy of Needs is 'belonging to a group'. This can result in clients using a strange language which only they, and other specialists, can understand. We do it ourselves. Our job is to translate these words into terms which the average reader will comprehend without effort.

Readers today have no patience. If they come across a word or phrase which is unfamiliar to them they are not likely to look it up – they will simply stop reading and move on, with fatal consequences for the success of our item. It pays to convert even the most complex client statement into language which a typical reader can follow without difficulty.

The only exception is when we know *for sure* that our media customers and their audience prefer technical jargon and use it themselves. This can be the case when we are targeting a very small, niche market, but it is rare for us to ignore the possibilities of a wider audience for our clients' media stories.

Haste: Hurrying obviously increases the probability of error. It also encourages us to deliver writing which is less than our best. 'I am sorry this letter is so long – I didn't have time to make it shorter'.

Information overload: This often happens when we are receiving our brief from more than one client contact. They all have vitally important points which *must* be included. The result, if we are unable to push back, can be a lengthy and over-complicated rendition of a simple story.

The ideal press-release is two pages at most – preferably one – and no more than 600 words. If you browse press rooms you will see 'press-releases' which go on for four, five or six pages. These do our media customers no favours – if they want the story they must spend time reducing the verbiage to its essential components. More likely, they will spike it in despair.

If they receive a simplified, terse version of our story, however, they can tell at a glance if they are interested and – if they want to know more – they can call or email the sender. But, with any luck, they will use the material we have sent them exactly as it stands.

PR people writing for the media score highly if the interests of their media customers and their own coincide – what we have sent appears without adaptation or reduction. When this happens, everyone is happy: editors save time and our clients are pleased.

Committee editing: This happens often and can be a real problem for PR people trying to provide the media with well-written, well-constructed material. It is triggered when our client contact sends the draft round to six, 12 or 24 colleagues for comment. Most people, if asked to comment, will comment.

What comes back to us is a camel.

What to do?

The best answer, not always practicable, is to encourage our client contact to review the draft alone. There may be corporate or personal reasons why he or she is unwilling to take this responsibility. Then we have to re-draft, as diplomatically as possible, and probably re-draft again, in a bid to arrive at something which will not make our media customers raise their eyebrows.

It can be particularly problematic if lawyers have been invited to comment. They always do, and it is never an improvement from the point of view of editorial quality.

If you browse pressrooms you will see example after example of 'media material' which has clearly been put together in order to satisfy a committee. It is not fit for purpose.

Push back, if you can. Clients and our own businesses pay us to know how to provide their stories to the media in a manner which the media will like. It doesn't make sense for clients to ignore our advice. Worse, if we send the media substandard material we are risking our own reputations as professionals – which, for most of us in PR, is our stock-in-trade.

Style

There is not much room for our own writing style in media material.

Unlike, for instance, our own blogs, stories, poems, lyrics, sketches, scripts and novels.

The objective is to convey information to our media customers as simply as possible. Terse, clear, unadorned. Not a word wasted. We want them to use it. If they choose to add colour this is up to them. It's not helpful if they have to edit or re-write to convert our material to their own house-style.

Here are some tips:

Well-worn phrases: Avoid. Bernard Kilgore, the famous managing editor of the *Wall Street Journal*, once sent a memo: 'If I read "upcoming" in the *WSJ* again, I shall be downcoming and someone will be outgoing'.

Clients often use terms like 'leverage' and 'leading'. It's best to find alternatives. If we pick up information from systems like Twitter and Linkedin (as we all do) it's easy to start using the 'word *du jour*' without even knowing we are doing so.

This has a deadening effect on our prose. The best defence is to ask someone else to check our copy before we send it out.

Using our own language, not theirs: Think of the reader we are aiming to engage. How do they speak? Probably not exactly like us. It makes sense to 'neutralise' the vocabulary and style of our media material. If that's impossible, it may be worth preparing two or three different versions of a story, each designed to match the natural language of its target audiences.

Passive voice constructions: Often used in corporate writing. 'It was decided that…' 'It became apparent that…' 'A consensus view was reached…' The passive voice reduces the dynamism and energy of our media material. Instead: 'The board agreed on a 20 per cent growth target for the coming financial year…' Even better: James Johnson, CEO, announced a 20 per cent growth target for the coming financial year – a 50 per cent increase on the target for the current year.

Interesting media writing is all about people doing things, saying things and thinking things. It makes sense to use the active voice whenever possible: he said this, they did that.

Adjectives and adverbs: Avoid unless you can't. Adjectives and adverbs are used to give colour to a narrative; most media material doesn't need colour, which gets in the way of telling the simple, nitty-gritty facts of our story. If the media want to liven up their version of our story they can add their own adjectives and adverbs. Usually, when they see them in a piece of PR material, they delete them.

Empty words and hype: Red rags to reporters, subs and editors. 'World's Leading' is so over-used that it became the ironic title of a PR website. Words like important, unique (or even worse, very unique), prestigious, game-changing, innovative, ground-breaking, inflection-point … and so on … raise the hackles of our media customers. If anyone is going to praise our clients it will be them, not us, and certainly not our clients themselves.

Quotations

These are incredibly important components of a good media story, yet editors tear their hair out at the diet of dull, robotic, corporate, legalistic quotes which the PR industry inflicts on them.

'Do PR companies exist because companies are led by individuals who have lost the capacity to speak in plain English?' asked Philip Delves Broughton in *The Telegraph*.

'Companies that understand the force of straight talking are so rare that we are astonished when we find them' said Simon Caulkin in the *FT*.

It's understandable. Most CEOs (not all) are nervous of the media. They retreat into a wooden form of self-expression when asked for a quote – safe, utterly risk free, and therefore boring.

Here is Jonathan Meades on jargon, quoted in *The Guardian* on 28 May 2018:

> *It is the prissy net curtains of language … centrifugal, evasive, drably euphemistic, unthreatening, conformist … jargon belongs to the executive suite … it is the clumsy, graceless, inelegant, aesthetically bereft expression of houses with three garages … delusional, inflates pomposity, officiousness and self-importance…*

I have heard from several editors that a vivid quote is so unusual that they will often publish a fairly so–so story just because they want to carry the quote. It makes sense to do everything we can to secure a company spokesperson's quote which is lively, interesting and sounds like a person.

'VW's problem is that they don't speak human' said Kamal Ahmed of BBC TV.

One strategy is to try to avoid email, which encourages 'what do you think' questions to colleagues and inevitably results in a committee product (a camel). Instead, see if you can arrange to speak to the source of the quote on the phone. Ask them to tell you, in their own words, just what is exciting, meaningful, important and significant about the topic of the story. They usually can – it's their job and they are normally completely wrapped up in it.

Make notes and then ask if you can ring back in 15 minutes to check your draft. Write a three-sentence quote capturing what they have said in vivid, everyday language. Then call them back and read it out: they will probably say: 'Yes – that's exactly what I said'. Bingo – you have a quote which will make an editor's eyes light up. It doesn't always work, but it's always worth trying.

Self-editing

Unlike our media customers, we don't have subs and editors to knock our writing into shape. This means we have to do it ourselves. The golden rule is to never, ever issue media material straight from the keyboard; always leave time for review between drafting and hitting the send button. This has a name: 'Pause and Return'.

Ideally, do something else for an hour or two before coming back to look at the draft.

Check the lead para: does it make *us* want to read on?

The theme: are we making a single point – a single message – in a single piece of text?

Length: trim by at least 10 per cent. Or, if you are like me, 20 per cent.

Direct speech: is the voice active? Does the writing come across as positive, dynamic?

Read it aloud (probably not in the office). The rhythms and emphases when we read aloud are usually different from those of a written text (scriptwriters confirm this) and can make us spot different ways of composing our copy more engagingly.

Ask a friend or colleague to criticise constructively. I have never issued a piece of media material without doing this and it *always* improves what I have written. In a way, this is our substitute for the subs who do the same thing to journalists' raw copy.

Read it backwards – starting with the last paragraph, ending with the first. This is useful in proofing; when we read according to the normal sense of a piece of text we don't actually read every syllable, so proofing our paragraphs in reverse will pick up mistakes we might not otherwise notice.

Structure: Are the paragraphs the right length? Are the cross-heads breaking up the text so as to make it more enjoyable to read? Does the text *look* right from a typographical point of view?

Spellcheck: Turn it off. Apart from UK/US differences, this will force us to examine every word.

Print it out: The way we consume material from a page is different from the way we consume it from a screen. Printing out our text helps us to think about it objectively.

Time is the enemy in most PR agencies and in-house teams. We always have too much to do. I suggest it is worth making our personal reputation with media customers our number one priority; it pays to take time and trouble to give them the best media material we can.

If the media think we know what they want and observe the same writing standards which they themselves consider important, it will make a big difference to the way they treat us. In their eyes we will rise above the mass of 'PRs' and start to be thought of as fellow professionals.

WHAT THE MEDIA WANT (AND DON'T WANT)

The news media today rely on PR agencies and PR departments for the majority of the material they publish. Most of the money that used to pay journalists' wages, which came from advertising, nowadays bypasses the media and goes straight to Google and Facebook. If you want to know why, read Ian Leslie's excellent analysis in the *New Statesman*: 'The Death of Don Draper' (25 July 2018).

Journalist numbers have shrunk. In 2002, there were around 70,000 editorial staff in the UK; today it is estimated that there are less than 25,000. At the same time PR employment has ballooned. The 2018 PRCA Census shows that there are now 86,000 of us.

You can see what's happening. For economic reasons, the provision of raw news material has swung away from the independent media towards people like us who are paid to issue certain kinds of information in a certain way.

The media depend on us. They don't like it very much, but there's no alternative.

As Basil Clarke and Anthony Hilton tell us, only one press release in a hundred will see the light of day – a percentage that has stayed surprisingly constant since the 1920s. But with 86,000 other PR people competing for a dwindling volume of editorial space and time, we can expect media success to get harder.

All the more reason to pay close attention to what our media customers want from us.

News. The media divide 'news' into *hard news* (we must cover this story), *soft news* (yes, if we have space or time) and *filler*. Beyond that there is just the spike, bin or delete key.

Hard news means mergers and acquisitions, senior appointments, important discoveries, major investments, financial results ... it also means closures, redundancies, crises and scandals.

Most of us, most of the time, have relatively little *hard news* to offer the media. As the old joke goes, the only time we can be sure of our client hitting the front page is when they have a crisis – the very time when we would prefer to keep them off it.

The exception is *celebrities*. For some reason famous names are always in the *hard news* category. This may prove the golden rule that all news stories are actually people stories.

Usually, our clients' stories are *soft news*. We will talk later about ways of making soft news items look 'harder'.

We should always bear in mind, though, that what our media customers *really* want from us is *hard news*.

Facts and figures. Most reporters remember the mortifying experience of having subs throw a story back at them because it lacks the facts and figures to make it 'stand up'. When we draft a story we must include (and start with) the who, what, when, where, why, how and how much.

The same applies when we are calling to place or 'sell-in' a story. Nothing annoys journalists more than a PR person who hasn't got the basic facts at their fingertips before picking up the phone. 'Oh, that might be interesting. So, what were the sales figures for 2017?' 'I'm sorry, I don't have that information. Can I get back to you?' This is not good PR but it happens all the time.

The media are not unreasonable. As Barry Fox said, they don't expect PR people to know everything. But they *do* expect us to know who does have the facts and figures, be able to get them and be able to convey them accurately. It's not much to ask.

Expert opinion. This is where PR people and journalists are on common ground. The media love debate, argument, controversy – even to the extent of what my editor called 'a punch-up on the page'. Some clients like expressing forceful opinions in public, but they're in a minority.

Even so, offering ideas, forecasts, warnings, points of view and divergent interpretations is one of the very best ways of achieving higher profile for our clients or employers and, at the same time, providing our media customers with material they actually want.

What if we have a client spokesperson who is nervous of the media, or just reluctant to speak out? There are two solutions. First, thorough media training: simulated interviews, captured on tape, nearly always lift clients' confidence and can sometimes transform a shy client into someone who can't wait to get into the studio.

It also helps if we make clients aware of interviews and commentary from their rivals. Senior people are, almost by definition, competitive. Seeing 'the enemy' achieving media success can inspire a media-averse client to get cracking.

If this doesn't work, are there other – less senior – people in the organisation who can act as media sources, and want to? There usually are. This is a good alternative if the organisation's protocol allows it.

It's worth pushing to get an authoritative, media-friendly spokesperson trained and ready to spring into action; I've met many PR people who sadly admit that they can't get their clients to talk to the media, which is like trying to run a PR programme with one arm tied behind your back.

Truth. Most business people exaggerate success and down-play failure – naturally enough. We expect it, and we automatically adjust what we hear. 'So, Caroline, how are sales going?' 'Fantastic – we're up 23 per cent on a like-for-like basis. It's going to be a great year!' What we hear is that things are going well, but we probably treat the 23 per cent figure with some scepticism.

It is fatal to massage facts and figures when our clients are speaking to the media. Only the unvarnished truth will do. If we – or our clients – lie to the media, and they find out, they will never forget it, and they will never trust us again.

Exclusives. All journalists want an exclusive – or a 'scoop' as the films about Fleet Street used to call them. There are two reasons: first, in an intensely competitive field an exclusive is a 'feather in the cap', a source of professional pride.

Second, it usually means a by-line. These matter a great deal to media writers. It's the only firm evidence that they wrote the story. Editors award by-lines sparingly, like medals.

We ring with a story and deliver our elevator pitch. 'Hmm ... that could be interesting. Is this just for me, or are you speaking to anyone else?' Tricky. How can we compare the impact of our story as an exclusive in a top outlet against that of widespread, if smaller, coverage across the sector? It's a judgement call, and never easy. We don't want to annoy the other fifteen writers on our A-List.

One solution is to offer each writer an exclusive *angle*. One gets a CEO interview, another gets a one-to-one with the head of research, another gets a visit to the laboratory. As long as each writer feels that he or she has a take on the story which is theirs and theirs alone, they will probably be happy.

Another solution is to operate a roster system. We can do this if our client or employer has a steady stream of announcements. We explain to our A-list that each will receive exclusive access to news items in turn. They don't like it very much – it smacks of 'news management' – but at least they can see that we are trying to be fair.

What if a journalist calls us about a story that we haven't yet released? In this case, all bets are off. The story belongs to them. It is an exclusive whether we like it or not.

To sum up: While the media are not 'feral beasts' as Tony Blair described them, they are highly competitive and they know precisely what they want. *Hard news*, first and foremost, ideally news that no-one else has uncovered. Second, combative statements from people in authority. Third, information or opinions which enable them to write a unique story.

Anything else is second best.

What the Media Say They Want and Don't Want from PR

Wants: quick descriptions, quotes, graphics
Doesn't want: convoluted text, long detail, unjustified claims
Alan Boyle (Neeley, 2012)

Wants: surprise, context, a 15-second pitch
Doesn't want: impenetrable language, obscurity
Bryn Nelson (Neeley, 2012)

Wants: precise, simple language
Doesn't want: exaggeration, rhetoric
Chris Joyce (Neeley, 2012)

Wants: the bigger picture; who did what?
Doesn't want: hype
Hilary Rosner (Neeley, 2012)

'If you're selling a story to a news organisation, use *news language*.'
Rod McKenzie (BBC News)

STORY INGREDIENTS: THE TREVOR MORRIS SYSTEM

One of the best ways to put together a news story comes from Trevor Morris, ex-CEO of Chime Communications and currently Professor of Public Relations at Richmond University. He calls it the 'story ingredients system'. The heart of the story is always: 'Who did it? Who will it affect?'

These are the ingredients:

The news: Problems, issues, conflict, controversy, drama, heroes and villains

The evidence: Facts, figures, references, graphics/infographics

The expert: Views, advice, comment, warning, urging, challenging, predicting

The example: Human interest case study, verbal illustration

The image: Photography, graphics

This system is a PR person's version of what journalists do when they are composing a story. Here are some suggestions on putting it into practice:

First, read the entire source documentation and highlight important words or phrases. If you meet an unfamiliar term or idea, explore on the web until you feel you understand the key points.

Second, compose a simple sentence which, you feel, sums up the point of the story. If this is difficult, consider whether or not there actually *is* a story in the material you are working on. If not, you are probably not doing your media customers any favours by persisting. Maybe you should advise your client or employer to wait until they have something genuinely newsworthy to offer.

What is *new*?
What is *different*?
What is the *change*? If there is no change, there is no story.

Third, choose your *story ingredients* from your source documentation and context research.

- *The news*: is a problem being solved?
  - Is an issue being pointed out or managed?
  - Is there controversy, conflict or debate?
  - Can you identify heroes (or villains)?
  - Is there drama? Is the story important?
- *The evidence*: Facts and figures to support what your story says
  - references from authoritative sources

- *The expert*: One or more people who are taking the leading role
  - challenging, urging, warning, predicting, advising, commenting
- *The example*: A picture of how the story affects people – or one person
  - can be real – historical or forecast – or hypothetical
- *The image*: Photographs, graphics, infographics, charts, maps, diagrams, sketches

Fourth, draft your first paragraph (the lead) and a headline (at this stage a working title)

Fifth, compose the rest of the story as a narrative: short words, short sentences, short paragraphs

Sixth, review what you have written. Ask someone else to read and comment

Seventh, leave the draft alone; do something else; come back later and re-read, re-edit

Eighth, reduce the total word count by 10 per cent and re-draft your headline

Yes, it takes a little longer than bashing out a piece of media material straight from the brief. Yes, this can be a trial when you have several of these to write today and the phones are ringing non-stop. And two meetings before you leave the office.

But it's worth it. Your own reputation with the media – and your agency's, your client's or your employer's – all depend on issuing top-quality media writing. That means material written in much the same way as your media customers would themselves write it.

It is better to issue *less* so that every item is the best you can possibly write.

WRITING FOR SCREENS – ADVICE FROM STEVE DUNNE

Steve Dunne is one of the UK's leading experts in digital communications. His company, Digital Drums, provides consultancy and tuition in creating compelling online content. Here are his tips on writing for screens:

Have you ever been told that online media require different writing skills from mainstream outlets? It's a myth. Exactly the same rules apply. The only difference is that it's much more difficult to capture and retain a reader's interest online, so your writing has to be even better.

Why is that? Most news is consumed on phones or tablets, so the reading experience encourages skimming. Mobile devices are just that – so your readers are probably looking at your material while they are doing something else: on a train, walking, in a meeting. Attention spans get shorter and shorter: down to somewhere between five and eight seconds on average.

We need to be even sharper and more ruthless with online content if we hope to get it read.

The headline is *all important*. Nearly 40 per cent of readers 'bounce off' the headline – in other words, they read no further.

Make your opening paragraph (the lead) enticing – who, what, when, where, why, how, how much.

Construct your story in 'chunks' – just as you do in writing for print, but more so. Online readers skip and skim, so they will rapidly decide if they want to read your item according to how easily they can grasp what it's about. And what's in it for them.

Half of online readers only read half of a typical story. How can we retain our readers' interest to the end? We can use illustrations (photographs, infographics) to defeat the 'wall of text' problem.

We can insert pull-quotes – gems which surprise and captivate our readers. We can make our cross-heads intriguing – not just a typographical break, as in print media, but a signpost to interesting information in the next paragraph.

We can use lists, which everybody loves, pulled out from the body copy and placed in a box.

We can use typographical devices (**bold,** *italic,* colour, CAPS) to highlight key points in our text. We can use punctuation to make our copy arresting (though we would rarely do this for a print outlet). We can insert links – but sparingly: links take readers away from our item and they might not come back.

Above all, we should bear in mind that online media are even more visual than print media. Readers expect pictures first and foremost. And not just pictures: clips and interviews which bring the story to life with a vivacity that copy cannot match, leaving our words to frame and explain like captions.

You may notice that Steve Dunne's recommendations make writing for screens sound a lot like writing advertising copy. In my opinion PR people have much to learn from copywriters – even though the advertising and PR industries have looked askance at each other for decades. This is even more salient at a time when PR is encompassing the whole PESO *(paid, earned, shared, owned)* communications channel model.

If you want a good example of an advertising copywriter who produces brilliant editorial, take a look at Dave Trott's blog (davetrott.co.uk) and tweets (@davetrott).

PITCHING A STORY TO THE MEDIA

We have written a great story. What next?

Some agencies and PR departments believe in the principle of 'spray and pray'. They think that issuing their stories to the largest possible number of potential writers will produce the highest number of media hits, and their client or employer will be happy. Their evaluation is probably based on 'opportunities to see', 'eyeballs' or 'hits'.

There is some truth in this. But not much. There is an 'iron law' in PR: the most influential outlets are the most difficult to engage. There is another, equally obvious rule: a story which all media want to carry does not require much skill on the part of a PR team. All companies, products and people have a natural level of media interest; our job is to get coverage *over and above* that level.

It pays, I suggest, to take more time and trouble. Pitch stories on the phone to your key media. They prefer it. Develop professional relationships with the media on your clients' A-lists. Know what they are writing and what they are likely to want. Ideally, know them personally.

As we move into a hyper-competitive PR era, with 86,000 PR people in the UK – all with the ability to email any given story to 200 media at once – it makes even more sense to pitch our stories to key journalists *personally*. Knowing how to do this successfully is what will distinguish us, and our agency, from the 'media mills'.

Here are some suggestions:

Journalists like to feel that they are being offered a story because the PR person believes it will appeal to them, personally. They hate – as we all do – being treated as just a name on a list. It makes sense to invest time in researching the journalist we are calling and working out a way of tailoring our sales-pitch to their interests *as an individual*. Remember that journalists are solo acts; they are highly competitive and have strong egos.

Step One: Make sure you know the story inside-out. Be confident that it really *is* a story. Learn (or note down) the 'fast facts' so that you are ready to answer obvious questions.

Know in advance your scope for offering the story as an exclusive, because you will very probably be asked. Know who has the in-depth information and that they will be happy to speak to the media. When are they available?

Most A-list journalists see PR people as channels (or barriers). They want to talk to the people who are at the centre of the story. We should be able to put the media in direct contact with an expert.

Acid Test: If you can't answer the media's questions yourself and you don't have an expert ready and willing, you should probably ask yourself if you should be pitching this story at all.

Step Two: Check that you have the right name and role for the journalist you are calling (they move around even faster than we do). The person who answers the desk or department phone will be happy to confirm this for you. They can also confirm something you probably already know: when, exactly, does this writer (or, in broadcast, researcher) like to be called with story ideas?

If you don't know the journalist and are working from a list, don't assume it's accurate. The media's Number One complaint about PR people is being pitched a story that they could not possibly be interested in covering ... it's a waste of time, obviously, but it's also insulting.

Your first call to a new media contact is incredibly important. They won't forget it. As Dale Carnegie said: 'You never get a second chance to make a good first impression'.

Step Three: Look at what the journalist has been writing over the last two or three months. Get a feel for their favourite topics, their point of view, who they seem to like as spokespeople, how happy they are to quite corporate sources (most are: some are not). Can you link your story to something they have been writing recently? If so, you have a marvellous opening line.

The more you know about the journalist you are calling, the happier they will feel and the more inclined they will be regard to you as a fellow-professional. This homework pays dividends.

Step Four: The call. A typical opening might be: 'Hello – is that Mr Smith? Oh, good – my name is Jane Jones and I am ringing on behalf of WAGS! Dogfood. I saw that you wrote a piece about the cost of pet-ownership last week and I think we have some new research results which might interest you. Is this a good time....?'

It is advisable to use formal salutations on your first call. Some journalists don't care, but some do.

Your opening has made it crystal-clear who you are, who you work for and why you are calling Mr Smith. You have got to the point straight away. The media complain about PR people who waffle, so avoid it. Don't forget to use the word 'new'. It has a magic effect on the *news* media.

Mr Smith will either say: 'Yes, so what's it about?' or 'No, I'm tied up at the moment.'

When would be a better time to call?

Mr Smith *may* ask you to send him the outline by email. If so (though this doesn't happen often) you should ask him what to put in the subject box. This is a necessary precaution: journalists receive so many emails that they simply don't have the time (or inclination) to read them all.

If he's interested, give Mr Smith your 'elevator pitch'.

This is a Hollywood expression meaning that you can sum up the key points of your story in 30 seconds or less. Some people can do this naturally, but most of us can't, so it's a good idea to write out these key points before you pick up the phone. It's a talent that comes with practice, but if you are doing your first media pitches rehearse what you intend to say with a colleague.

Mr Smith may say: 'Thanks, but I don't think that one's for me'. If so, terminate the call politely: 'OK – thank you for listening – I hope my next story will be more to your liking'. Whatever you do, don't try to argue or persuade journalists to change their mind – they really hate it.

With any luck, Mr Smith will say: 'Hmm. Tell me a bit more about it. How many dog owners did you talk to?' Or something like that. This is where you must know your facts. Journalists expect you to know the answers to basic questions before you call them.

Mr Smith may ask about exclusivity. You should already know if you are authorised to agree an exclusive with any particular writer on your A-list. If so, you can reasonably expect larger and more in-depth coverage. If not, you should say so openly – but maybe you can offer Mr Smith a substitute? A special angle on the story, an interview with WAGS!'s head of research, a one-to-one with a dog-owner from your research sample...

Whatever you agree, the call will usually end with Mr Smith asking you to send more information. Remember to ask him what you should put in the subject box. Give him your 24 × 7 number.

To chase or not to chase? What if Mr Smith doesn't call back, doesn't reply to your email and seems to have lost interest? The rule of thumb is to leave it with him for a day and then – if you hear nothing – send a polite enquiry, using the same subject-box title, saying that you are assuming he has decided not to pursue the story. If nothing happens after that, move on. Remember that only one story in a hundred makes it all the way to publication.

It sometimes happens that Mr Smith *was* interested, asked questions, interviewed the head of research, asked you for special pictures ... and nothing appeared. This is because journalists often write material which gets canned for reasons of space or time. If this happens Mr Smith will be as disappointed as you are, and will tell you so next time you buy him a drink.

This may seem like a lot of work. It is certainly more time-consuming than just pumping stories out to a list. But it's worth it. You are treating your media customers as individuals, which they obviously prefer; you are also building the foundations of *real* media relationships – getting to know your A-list and letting them get to know you.

MAKING A 'SOFT' STORY STRONGER

The media have a specific definition of a news story. It's *new*, it's about *change* and it's *important*. Above all it involves *human interest* – all news stories are human-interest stories.

It's obvious that what the media like best of all is bad news. 'Bad news is good news'. Disasters, scandals and ruined reputations raise circulation. Equally obviously, what we proactively offer the media is always 'good news' – which normally falls into the category of 'nice to have'.

There are steps we can take to make a soft story stronger in the eyes of our media customers.

Human interest. Who made it happen? How and why? Who will it affect? Many people? Can we extrapolate? Will all our lives improve? If we use our imagination, even a fairly humdrum trade story can turn into an interesting narrative with far-reaching implications. I am not advocating hype, but it's worth thinking about the back-story and the effects. What led up to this change? How, exactly, is it innovative? What are the consequences for human beings?

Public interest. The media think of themselves as champions of the public interest – as indeed they are. Can we frame our story as a step taken in the interests of the general public? Will it lead to better health, lower emissions, greater protection, a fairer deal? Is it in line with the three Ps – people, profit and planet? In my opinion Sir Paul Polman has made Unilever far more attractive to the media by espousing a 'higher cause' for this giant FMCG company. Most journalists are much more interested in *people* and *planet* than profit (unless they work for the *FT*).

Topicality. Can we link our story to a calendar event? This automatically gives it more of a news flavour. Are we releasing it in the 'week of' or the 'day of'? Is there an anniversary we can cite? Logically or not, tying our story to a day, a week, a month or a year increases its news value.

Quotations. Good quotes are rare in PR. For this reason, a vivid quote can lift a story from 'spike' to 'nice to have' and even from 'nice to have' to 'must use'. Journalists love spokespeople who talk like human beings and are not afraid of expressing some kind of emotion in their statements. A good quote can make all the difference to pick-up, so it's worth going to great lengths to get spokespeople to say interesting things in an interesting way. Most people can do this when they're talking to their friends, so it's not impossible to put the same kind of vigour into a press release.

Response. One of the best ways to lift the news value of a story is to frame it as a response to something that is already in the news – a trend, a theme, a meme. The media like it. In fact, this is a great way to secure coverage when we have no *news* other than the expression of our client's or organisation's opinion on a topic of current media interest.

Conflict. Another media favourite. Sometimes called *debate* or *balance*. Journalists like to present an opposing view – if they can get one – so a very good way of making our story stronger is to present it as contrarian – a dissenting opinion which takes issue with the conventional line. Some clients are cut out for this; they have strong views and like to get stuck into arguments. If you are lucky enough to have this kind of spokesperson the media will beat a path to your door.

DISTRIBUTION: THE PESO MODEL

Not long ago clients saw PR firms and in-house teams as being dedicated mainly or solely to handling relationships with the media – or, more prosaically, getting as much positive media coverage as possible. That was it.

Today it is still true that most PR people spend at least half their time producing material for the media and doing their best to get it published. But times have moved on.

PR agencies and departments now have many more channels of communication with stakeholders available to them: *paid, earned, shared, owned.*

Clients today think of the *origination of content* (writing!) as central to their communications investments. This is where most of them see the special value of public relations practitioners.

They are right. Originating stories is where PR people excel. Media content is the *only* thing that *only* we do properly.

Choosing and using a variety of channels, outlets, vehicles and platforms is the natural next step once we have generated our core content. This is often the most 'creative' aspect of planning a PR programme. It makes sense to keep the different 'media' opportunities in mind while we are composing our media material.

- *Paid media*: Advertising (corporate, trade, consumer); sponsored editorial; inserts, sponsored posts and tweets; influencers; sponsorships (events, sports, arts, awards, etc.); and so on.
- *Earned media*: This category is 'traditional PR'. TV, radio, newspapers and magazines (General Interest and Special Interest); posts on third-party blogs; conference speeches; quotations in journals and books; any outlet where our

material will *earn* publication by virtue of its intrinsic interest and – of course – the skill with which we have presented it.

- *Shared media:* Online and social. They don't 'belong' to anybody. They are not governed or – for the most part – edited. Obviously extremely important today and more so in future. What's the catch? Volume. With millions of posts, discussion-thread contributions and vlogs being published every day, we are up against massive competition in the battle to get noticed. What's the solution? Follow Steve Dunne's advice. If we can't think up a great headline we are sunk.
- *Owned media*: Sometimes called *captive media*. Our own (or our clients') websites, internal magazines/wikis/intranets; FB pages; twitter accounts; Town Hall meetings; open days; and so on. We control what is said and how it is said. A dream ticket? Not really; we can't assume that control equates to readership. The reverse is often the case. As a rule of thumb, what we publish in *owned media* needs to be more engaging than the content we deliver via *earned* and *shared*.

A final point when we are distributing the same story through PESO. Think about the readers. They will usually be different people, with different 'media consumption' habits and different natural preferences when it comes to vocabulary and style. Should we compose different versions of the same story for each target audience? Probably, yes. More work!

APPENDIX

ADVICE FROM JOURNALISTS AND EDITORS

Tips for Better Coverage

Pictures can often be the deal-breaker for regional media. They are short of resources. It is often the release with a picture that makes the cut. Pictures should be interesting – *not* people shaking hands, cutting ribbons or grinning inanely at the camera.

TV. More valuable, more demanding. For instance, if your story is about record-breaking apricot crops the footage could be drone clips of the orchards – rather than warehouses full of boxes.

Selling in: get to the point. I am busy. Don't witter about holidays or the weather – and never, ever, call me 'mate'. Does this happen?, you ask. Yes! We all hate it.

Timing: don't call when I am on deadline. How do you know? It's obvious: ring the desk beforehand and find out when journalists like to receive calls from PR people.

If I ask for further information – and, if I'm interested, I usually do – ring back when you said you would. It's amazing how often PR people 'forget'. If you are that kind of PR person don't be surprised if I am a bit short next time you call me.

Regional media: we still have 1,100 regional dailies and weeklies in the UK. It's an important sector. If you are calling the regional media, make sure there is a local angle.

Copy approval: Some PR people ask for this. Fair enough if you are working in Saudi Arabia. In the UK it's an affront. Don't.

Contact availability: I am constantly amazed when PR people pitch a story without anyone lined up for me to talk to. Remember that you are a *channel* – an intermediary between me (the writer) and the person who can give me information, answer questions and come up with quotable quotes.

Phone numbers: Never send me anything without giving at least one phone number. You may live on email – we don't. Talking to the source is all-important. At least, it is when you are offering your story to a real journalist. If you're not... what exactly are you doing for your client?

Iain McBride is a veteran newspaper, TV and radio journalist. He has also worked in PR.

What I Want from You

Recognise that I am usually working to a quick turn-around deadline, so *clarity* is imperative. What is the news in your story? I want the USP, the context, facts and quotes from significant authorities.

I need you to be aware of the different slots in the newspapers/magazines/websites/social media outlets that I am writing to fill. It could be a diary item, a comment piece, a news story, a feature; it could appear in the news section or the business pages, lifestyle or sport. You might be surprised how often a story can cross over from one area to another.

When I am writing features, I need all of the above but something else as well: I want my own angle, to suit my publication. It helps if you have already thought about how *your* story could be *my* story.

A magazine or feature piece has a longer shelf-life on people's coffee-tables, tablets and memories, so I am looking for a more personalised 'experiential' opportunity from my PR contact. It could be an exclusive one-to-one interview or a tour behind the scenes; the *first* sampling of an experience or a new product ... I have to assure my editor that this is either an opportunity for us to be first or that it's a real exclusive. A scoop!

Social media: *Filmable* is tops. Snapchattable. Instagrammable moments. Social is very immediate for the consumer but needs a lot of planning on the part of the editorial team. The earlier a PR contact can share a timetable of potential live events or appearances the better. Also ... is there scope for behind-the-scenes coverage? Think Wimbledon!

Sarah Edworthy is a news and feature writer for the nationals, currently working at Vanity Fair/Tatler

The 'Story Ingredients' System

When you sit down to write a media story it can sometimes be helpful to use a pattern. Most journalists do this, consciously or not. The 'Golden Rule' is that *all* media stories are *people* stories – even if your client thinks they're about batteries, ships or derivatives.

The news: What is different? What's changed or about to change? Is a problem being solved, an issue tackled, a conflict dealt with, a controversy fuelled? Is there drama? Who are the heroes or villains?

The evidence: Media stories have to 'stand up'. This means facts and figures – not airy claims. What references do you have to hand? Graphics and infographics? Statistics? Third-party corroboration?

The expert: A spokesperson who talks in short, everyday words. An authority. Opinions, advice, warnings, challenges, contrarian views, predictions. Are they urging people to do something? Are they recommending that the government takes action?

The example: Here is the human interest. A case-study (historical) or a future projection. A real person, family, neighbourhood, club, company … use verbal illustrations and quotations to bring this part of the story to life.

The image: Pictures, clips, graphics. We live in a visual age. Most media think 'online first' which means good quality images – not stock-shots and not brochure pictures. Bring in a professional media photographer/video expert – they are worth their weight in gold.

The acid test: So what? If it's hard to answer this question, maybe you should think again about issuing the story. Our media customers get 400 a day and most are deleted. Think about your target – in the first place it's a journalist or an editor. What's special about your item? What makes it stand out? Don't send six 'stories' a month just because your client wants you to: try to make a name for yourself as someone who offers the media material they can actually use.

Trevor Morris was CEO of Chime Communications and is now Professor of PR at Richmond University

How to Make Me Like You

It's tough being a journalist. Most of us get too many press releases, most of us don't have much job security, deadlines are tight and getting tighter. Most publishers these days downplay quality reporting and feature-writing in favour of volume and clickable links.

So ... if you want me to respond well to your pitch or press release, have some sympathy.

Think about how you can make me like you more – and how to make me look more favourably on your communications in the future.

Don't waste my time: Most journalists get at least 50 emails a day; a busy freelancer will get over 400. They won't all be press releases – there will be blog notifications, newsletters, even messages from actual people. Make my life easier … don't send me irrelevant stuff, don't send marketing waffle that I will have to strip out of the story. Make sure the subject line tells me whether I need to open the message and read on. Put all the key facts up front. Include links to downloadable images.

Talk to me: Customise! This means knowing something about *me* – what I write and how I write. Who I write for. Your covering note for a press release should be personalised, flagging up the particular elements of the story that might appeal to *me*.

Or give me some information that no-one else is getting (at least, not without asking for it). Or offer me the story in advance of everyone else – put an embargo on it, but at least give me a head-start on my competition. There is way too much competition for the average journalist, so help me feel good about myself because you rate my contribution.

Spell my name right. It's so easy to get a name, title or even a publication wrong if you're sending the same pitch to multiple outlets ... this is guaranteed to make me (and everyone else) cross.

Respond: If I ask for more information, acknowledge the request and then get it to me ASAP. If the client won't play ball, bite the bullet and tell me. If you leave me dangling, you and your agency will lose my respect – so I'll be disinclined to read your emails first in future.

Exclamation marks: Noooooooooo. Ditto mis-spellings, and ALL CAPS anywhere in the communication. The same applies to (gulp) fancy formatting including odd fonts. But you would never do that, would you?

Dennis Jarrett is an Editor, Writer, Author and Conference Speaker, latterly working in Dubai.

FIVE TOP TIPS

The notion of press relationships seems to be ignored by vast swathes of your industry. I sometimes wonder what clients are paying you for.

Kamal Ahmed, BBC Economics Editor

We don't expect PR people to have all the answers. What we expect is that they can get the answers and give them to us quickly and accurately.

Barry Fox, *New Scientist*

It's nice when they get my name right. It doesn't happen often.

Dennis Jarrett, Freelance journalist

Treat the media like customers or clients. They are not machines, numbers or names on a list. If you approach them as individuals (most PR people don't bother) they will prefer to work with you and your clients ... human nature.

Nicholas Watson, *Business New Europe*

Call first. Don't just "spray and pray". Time-consuming, but worth it. "I saw you were writing about the costs of nuclear energy last week, so I thought you might be interested in a new study from our client ABC Reactors ..." If they are, hooray! But, even if not, they will remember you as someone who knew something about them. This matters.

Euan Edworthy, CEO, Best Communications

BOOKS ABOUT THE MEDIA AND MEDIA WRITING

The best way to acquire and hone media writing skills is to read the best media writing. If you are a 'media junkie' this is easy.

The best way to understand the working environment and motivation of our media customers is to have worked in the media yourself, or to have friends who are journalists.

They inhabit a strange world. It is unlike ours. It is often said that reporters and journalists resemble each other more than any of them resemble us.

These books provide an insight into what it's like to be a journalist and what it's like to work in the media – a 'carnival of insecurity' according to Andrew Marr, whose book *My Trade* is required reading for anyone who is serious about their career in PR.

Flat Earth News	Nick Davies
Hack Attack	Nick Davies
Good Times, Bad Times	Harold Evans
The Journalist's Handbook	Kim Fletcher
Bad Science	Ben Goldacre
A Hack's Progress	Phillip Knightley
My Trade	Andrew Marr
The Universal Journalist	David Randall
A Crooked Sixpence	Murray Sayle
Tabloid Secrets	Neville Thurlbeck
The Media Moguls	Michael Wolff

Where do you find the best media writing? It's a matter of opinion, of course. Here's mine:

The Guardian

The New York Times

The Economist

Fortune Magazine

Scientific American

The New Yorker

Vanity Fair

Atlantic Monthly

IMPROVING YOUR MEDIA WRITING

Always ask someone else to look at your draft before you send it out. This is a religion for me and people like me: we don't have subs or editors, so we need another set of eyes – usually a colleague's – to make sure that what we've written is interesting, cogent and well-constructed.

Hand on heart, I can say that nothing I have ever written has not been improved by the comments of a friend or colleague. No-one enjoys criticism, but in the case of media writing it pays dividends.

Leave a gap between drafting your copy and sending it. There is nothing worse, from the point of view of quality, than issuing your work as soon as you have completed it. Of course, this can be difficult when you are snowed under. But what matters more? Pushing stuff out or making a name for yourself as the author of good media material?

Keep a scrapbook. Journalists do. You can look back at what you wrote three years ago and feel pleased at how much better your writing has become. Alternatively ... but we hope not.

Write on your own account. You may naturally want to, though most people in PR don't. It's worth a try: your own blog, your own website (think of Rich Leigh) or maybe just contributions to other people's online outlets ... the point is that writing over your own name will give you a useful insight into what it's like to be a journalist.

Be ruthless. If in doubt, out. There is (obviously) far more media material out there than can possibly be absorbed. It has been estimated that every adult in Western Europe receives 4,000 messages a day through their eyes and ears. Only the very best has any chance of being seen, read and acted upon. We should all be our own brutal editors.

Above all ... read good media writing. You may be lucky enough to have been born with a natural talent. But most of us weren't, so our best strategy is to learn by example. Read as much good media material as you can, as often as you can.

Bit by bit, the techniques and style of the masters – the Marrs, Liddles, Hydes and Gordons – will influence the way you see the 'hook' of a story, develop it, add colour, pick quotes, bring the narrative to life ... and make your own media writing something that people want to talk about during 'water-cooler' conversations.

A SELECTION OF JOURNALISM TERMS

Above the fold	Top half of page; more prominent, more valuable
ABC	Audit Bureau of Circulation: authentic sales figures
Advertorial	Resembles editorial but paid for; normally says so clearly
Advocacy journalism	When a reporter takes sides in a controversial issue
Ambush	Pouncing on someone who does not expect to be interviewed
Anchor	Newscasters who host news broadcasts regularly
Angle	Approach or focus of a story; also known as the peg
AP	Associated Press: media-owned wire service
Assignment	Work given to a reporter by an editor
Astroturfing	Fake grass-roots support, usually via websites, blogs, social media

Atmos	Atmosphere; aka actuality, ambient sound in radio and TV items
Attribution	Reference to original source of quote, facts, data
B copy	Bottom section of a story written in advance
B-roll	File or stock footage shown behind a reporter or over their words
Background (BG)	Explanatory information given to a reporter
Back bench	Senior editors on a title
Banner	Big headline; aka ribbon, streamer, screamer
BARB	TV audience measurement system
Beat	Subject regularly covered by a reporter; aka patch, round
Blurb	Brief introduction to writer, usually after headline
Box	Short item highlighting aspect of story; aka breakout
BRAD	Source of data for periodicals carrying advertising
Break	When a story is first published
Breaking news	Unexpected developments. Good for TV, inconvenient for print
Buried lede	Key element of article mistakenly hidden in the text
Byline	Writer's name displayed at start of story
Caption	Short description of picture; aka cutline
Churnalism	Practice of re-hashing press releases (derogatory)

CVI	Centre of Visual Interest on a page – usually a headline or picture
CIOJ	Chartered Institute of Journalists
Circulation	Number of copies sold (ABC). Not *readership*
Citizen journalism	Public reporting of news, usually on sites, blogs or social networks
Civic media	Outlets designed to encourage community awareness
Clip	Video or film footage from a few seconds to 10 minutes
Close-up, C/U	Subject's face fills the screen
Closed question	Interview question discouraging anything other than 'yes' or 'no'
Column	A regular feature, usually on a specific topic, by the same writer
Copy	The main text of a story, material for publication
Copy approval	A source or interviewee allowed to check the story draft
Copy editor	A sub who corrects reporters' material before publication
Copy taster	Senior sub-editor who filters incoming material
Correspondent	Specialist writer. May or may not work in the office
Cover-shot	Establishes place, location before TV news item begins
Cover story	The leading story, featured on the front cover
Crop	Cut or mask unwanted parts of a photograph

Crosshead	Line breaking up blocks of text. Same as sub-head
Cub	Junior or trainee reporter; aka rookie or junior reporter
Cue sheet	Script and information for radio reporters/presenters
Cutaway	Transition shot linking two themes: avoids jump-cut
Cuttings job	Article put together from existing material (derogatory)
Dateline	Gives date and location at the start of a story
Deadline	Time when reporter must finish an assignment
Deck	Also 'dek' or 'bank'. Summary of story under headline
Direct quote	Verbatim quotation in quotation marks
Draft	First version of a piece before submission to editor
DPS	Double-page spread
Drop intro	Or 'delayed intro'. Main point comes after first sentence
Endnote	Text after article stating author's credentials
Ends	Traditional indication of end of copy
Exclusive	Item published first in one outlet. Same as scoop
Fact-checker	Editorial staffer who verifies information before publication
Feature	Longer, more in-depth article, usually emphasising human aspects

File	To send in a story, usually by phone or email
Filler	Soft material used to fill space
Flash	Short item on a news event
Flatplan	Page plan showing shape and size of articles, pictures and ads
Folo	Story that follows up on a news story theme
Freelancer	Writer who sells to various media outlets
Freesheet	Title supported entirely by advertising revenue
FX	Sound effects added after initial recording
Geotag	Label identifying source of online content
Get	A very good or exclusive interview
Graf	Paragraph
Hard news	Live and current news in contrast to features
Hed	Headline (HTK – headline to come)
HFR	Hold for release. Same as embargo
Hook	The key element in a news item – what attracts interest
House style	Outlet's rules for punctuation, spelling, grammar, usage
Insert	Material placed between blocks of copy in a story
Intro	All-important first para; aka intro, lead or lede
Jumpline	Indication that article continues on a later page

Kicker	First part of story's lead, set in larger type
Legacy media	Aka mainstream media or MSM
Literal	Mistake; aka typo
Lobster shift	Working in the hours after publication
Long-lead	Magazines which commission items months in advance
Long-shot	TV picture framing that shows the scene of the event
Markup	Sub-editor's instructions on changing and laying-out copy
Masthead	Title section at front or top of media outlet
More follows	Or m/f. Tells sub story is not complete
Morgue	Traditional name for newspaper library
Mug-shot	Head-and-shoulders portrait, facing camera
NCTJ	National Council for the Training of Journalists
News agency	Company generating and selling material to media
NIB	News in Brief – quick summary of a story
Noddy	Separately taped footage of interviewer listening
Nut graf	Paragraph containing essential elements of a story
NUJ	National Union of Journalists
Off-diary	Unscheduled story. As opposed to on-diary
Off the record	Material which a reporter agrees not to use

On the record	Information which can be used in an article
Op-ed	Opinion piece by journalist or outside contributor
Pan	Moving the camera from left to right or right to left
Par	Paragraph
Pitch	Story idea presented to editor by reporter or other source
Pix	Pictures, photographs
Pool	A limited number of media share material with others
PPA	Periodical Publishers' Association
Puff piece	News item with complimentary tone or statements
Pulitzer Prize	Fourteen journalism prizes awarded by Columbia University
Pull-quote	Quote highlighted next to main text; aka lift-out quote
Redletter	Exclusive, breaking news printed in red type
Reported speech	Non-verbatim account of what someone said
Retraction	Withdrawal of published fact or story
Roundup	A story pulling together various related items
Rowback	Correction which does not admit to being a correction
Run	To publish a story
Sidebar	Story elaborating aspects of a story nearby

Scoop	An exclusive
Segue	Uninterrupted transition from one TV scene to another
Slant	Writing to influence reader's opinion; angle
Soft news	Interesting or entertaining, but not important
Sound-bite	The taped quote in a TV or radio news item
Source	An individual who provides information for a story
Spike	Where rejected copy was impaled: to spike a story means 'kill it'
Splash	Front page story
Standfirst	Line of text after headline giving more information about the item
Strapline	Similar to a stand first or a sub-head (more common in advertising)
Stringer	Irregular contributor, paid per story or by lineage
Sub-editor	Person who checks reporter's text, adds headlines and crossheads
Subhead	Crosshead
Throw	One person on air hands over to another
Thumbnail	Small-format photograph
Tick-tock	Step-by-step account of a news event's development
Tie-in	Placing a news story in context of past events; aka tie-back
Tip	A lead or piece of new information, often given confidentially

Verification	System checking truth of what reporter has been told
Verso	Left-hand page. Recto: right-hand page
Wire service	News service like AP or United Press
WOB	White text on black background

STORY PLATFORMS

If you are trying to figure out how to package a 'soft' news item, this is a list of the most common forms used by the media to present stories. Dissemination through owned and paid media can lead to earned and shared media exposure if the presentation makes the most of relatively weak content.

Topics

Advice

Anniversaries

Awards

Bids or tenders

Calendar events

CSR initiatives

Celebrities

Conferences, symposia

Customers, clients

Employee activities

Employment, jobs

Events

Exhibitions

Expansion

Expert opinion

Financial results

Forecasts, predictions

Improvements

Inventions, innovations

Investments

Management appointment

Mergers, acquisitions

New brand, logo, name

New contracts

New premises

New processes

New products

New services

Orders

Promotions

Reports, research studies

Speeches

Sponsorships

Surveys

Warnings

Frameworks

Animals

Arguments, debates

Challenges to orthodoxy

Change the world

Children

Competitions

Corrections

Employees

Environment

Factoids

Families

Human interest

Humour

Link to forthcoming date

Link to news agenda

Link to specific published story

Man bites dog (reversal)

Odd, unusual

Profile of person, team

Profile of organisation

Quirky angle

Quotable opinion

Sand to Saudis (unexpected)

Slow news days

Sustainability

Update

Formats

Advertorials

Backgrounders

Briefings

Cartoons

Case studies

Columns

Down-the-line

Exclusives

Facebook page item

Facility visits

Features

Fledgling sessions

Freelance assignments

Graphics, infographics

Interviews, one-to-ones

Letters to the editor

News features

News releases

Op-eds

Photo-ops

Picture-stories

Premieres

Press conferences (rarely)

Press launches

Press previews

Press receptions

Press room items

Press trips

Radio news releases

Site visits

Special reports, supplements

Spokespeople

Tweets

VNRs

White papers

Wire stories

YouTube clips

Putting it into Practice

Here are some exercises based on the recommendations given in this book:

Headlines and Leads

Caxton's 'Marathon' Launch. Our client is Caxton, a minnow in the office printer sector which sees itself as a Dyson. Its customers are split between corporates, SMEs and home-office users. Caxton is up against giants like HP, Lexmark, Canon and Epson.

Its new product – Marathon – has a USP. Its ink cartridges last twice as long as anyone else's but cost the same. Caxton thinks this will be a big selling-point in a market where customers resent the frequency and price of cartridge replacement. There is a downside: the Marathon printer costs twice as much as anything similar on the market.

Caxton is sure customers will be happy to pay more upfront in return for lower running-costs.

Caxton's marketing manager thinks this innovation deserves wall-to-wall coverage – not just the trades but nationals too ... and why not TV?

Challenge: Draft the headline and lead for the launch release.

Neutraceuticals and New Mothers. A team in Canada has conducted a survey of 41 new mothers in their 20s and 30s to see if diet supplements could have a beneficial effect on their mood – specifically, to see if they could alleviate postnatal depression.

It is thought that a sudden post-partum decline in sex hormones can trigger a rise in monoamine oxidase A, which can break down dopamine and serotonin.

Three-quarters of women experience the 'baby blues' in the first week following birth. It usually fades but one in eight new mothers' experiences post-natal depression.

Half the mothers in the study were given a daily dose of blueberry juice with 2 g of tryptophan and 10 g of tyrosine starting three days after giving birth. The others were given nothing.

Depression rates among the 'nothing' group rose swiftly. In the 'dose' group there was none at all.

Challenge: Write the headline and lead for the announcement.

Superwings' New Plane. We are XMP, manufacturers of a specialised polypropylene called 'Epron', which is very light but extremely strong. It is used in cars and boats to provide shock-absorbency and insulation. Epron is everywhere but invisible. We want to emulate Intel by creating a stronger public profile for Epron.

A great opportunity has come our way. Superwings, an experimental aircraft company, has invited XMP to partner with it in the production of a prototype aeroplane powered by the sun's energy. It will be ultra-light because it will use Epron for its fuselage, spars and wings.

The prototype – MITHRAS – will be able to carry six passengers for up to 1,000 km using solar power alone. Superwings sees a terrific future for its design concept in the passenger aircraft sector. We see a great opportunity for Epron to become a brand with consumer recognition.

MITHRAS has passed its initial flight-worthiness tests but has received virtually no media attention as yet. We are planning a grand media day at Biggin Hill where TV, radio and reporters will witness MITHRAS performing its first flight in public.

Challenge: Write the headline and lead for the press release.

A New SUV from Riley. Our client is Riley Cars, a private-equity-backed flag-bearer for the revival of the British car industry. Based in Coventry, Riley has been achieving sales success and excellent reviews for its up-market saloons and coupes. It competes head-on with BMW and Mercedes.

Riley's corporate USPs are its CEO – Mike Parker – a highly respected veteran of the European quality car industry; and its design team, who are all from the racing and high-performance sector. The company is a favourite of the media, the government and of course regional politicians. It has an enviable record for industrial relations.

We are launching Riley's new model, an SUV with the safety of a Volvo and the performance of a Porsche. It offers terrific value for money. Riley think the combination of value, safety and performance – plus the patriotic factor – will carve out a big niche in the SUV/crossover sector.

The R6 will appeal, in Riley's opinion, to both male and female owners. It can do everything required of a family car but it also has genuine off-road capability, impressive acceleration, a distinctive 'Riley' design and the cachet of being designed and made in Britain.

Challenge: Write the headline and lead for the launch press release

Alistair Osborne and BT. Alistair Osborne in the *Times* of 11 May 2018 was not impressed by a BT headline:

'And all wrapped up in some "transformational" waffle headlined: "BT announces strategy update to drive leadership in converged connectivity and services". Yeah, whatever'.

Challenge: Re-write the headline to avoid Mr Osborne's sarcasm.

Vivid Quotes

Aga Saga. Aga, the traditional British cooker/oven manufacturer, has been acquired by an American company, Middleby. Its chairman and CEO said:

> *We believe this transaction will provide meaningful growth opportunities as we leverage Aga's existing sales, service and manufacturing capabilities with Middleby's market expertise, product innovation and well-established global distribution network.*
>
> *Challenge: Re-write the quote to make it less corporate and more compelling*

A Convoluted Quote.

> *The transition to an on-demand digital environment requires a shift to an asset-centric approach to media asset management, capturing meta-data at the outset of the asset's life-cycle. This in turn enables greater movement and sharing of audio and visual material across the network to deliver increased exploitation of assets.*

Challenge: Re-write this quote to make it comprehensible and interesting

Google and Novartis. Google announced a partnership with Novartis to develop 'smart contact lenses' able to monitor glucose levels in diabetes patients. Sergey Brin said:

Our dream is to use the latest technology in the miniaturisation of electronics to help improve the quality of life for millions of people. We are excited to work with Novartis to make this dream come true.

Challenge: Can you improve this quote?

Peter Polymer of XMP. XMP's CEO is Peter Polymer, a chemical engineer. We have asked him for a quote to include in our release announcing the partnership between Superwings and XMP to develop a prototype solar-powered aircraft. He sends us this:

I am delighted to announce this innovative joint-venture between XMP, the world's leading supplier of ultra-strong thermoplastics, and Superwings. It is no over-exaggeration to say that this unique partnership offers remarkable benefits over traditional aeronautical design paradigms. We are confident in anticipating significant opportunities for our customers and excellent returns for our investors.

Challenge: Re-write Peter Polymer's statement to make it more vivid

A Great Story from WAGS! Dogfood. Our client, WAGS! Dogfood, has surveyed 2,000 dog owners and discovered that over half of them said they preferred their dog to their spouse. We think this is a great story and have asked Arthur Airedale, the CEO, for a quote. We get this:

> *The role of well-balanced nutrition in ensuring a long and healthy life for a dog cannot be over-stated. The mission of everyone at WAGS! Dogfood is to make a well-designed and scientifically-proven canine diet available for dog-owners everywhere, with affordability a priority. The results of this survey only go to underline the importance of diet in making sure that owners and their dogs are able to enjoy a long and happy life together.*

> *Challenge: Can we make Airedale's quote add colour to the story?*

A Tragedy Involving BMW. A former Ghurka died as the consequence of an electrical fault in a BMW. A BMW spokesperson said:

> *We extend our heartfelt sympathies to the family of Mr Gurung. As this matter is still the subject of court proceedings, we are unable to comment specifically on it.*

> *Challenge: Re-write the quote to convey a stronger sense of empathy*

A Crisis for Save the Children. Not long after the Oxfam scandal hit the front pages a similar tale of alleged misdeeds put Save the Children in the media spotlight. Their statement said:

> *We denounce Rudy von Bernuth's actions prior to and during his employment at Save the Children before his termination in 2014. We are heartbroken at the pain he caused.*
>
> *Challenge: Re-write this statement to sound less corporate and more human*

A Scandal at the National Dogger Bank. The National Dogger Bank ('NatDog') has still not recovered from investigations into its activities during the financial melt-down in 2007/2008. The bank's reputation is at rock-bottom. Now a fresh scandal has emerged: a rogue trader, Maximilian Martian, who has been systematically misleading investors. Repairs could cost the NatDog billions. The bank's CEO says:

> *We profoundly regret the consequences of Mr Martian's unauthorised activities and will co-operate with the authorities in ensuring full restitution to those investors affected. I would like to assure the bank's shareholders that this was a one-off in the full sense of the term and should be understood to imply no deficiencies whatsoever in the National Dogger Bank's oversight and compliance systems.*
>
> *Challenge: Make the CEO's statement more credible*

MEDIA QUOTES ABOUT THE MEDIA

The media are the root of consensus, the organisational motor of society. They are a more influential force in our lives and in the world's changing beliefs than politics or governments ever were.

Michael Wolff, *The Autumn of the Moguls (2010)*

I am a journalist, brought up to challenge authority, to contest the official version of events, to stand outside the establishment.

Simon Kelner, *iNews (2016)*

Reporters run on a volatile mixture of imagination and anxiety – like petrol and air.

Nick Davies, *Hack Attack (2015)*

In journalism, panic is *the system.*

Lynn Barber, *Demon Barber (1998)*

Conflict, drama and setbacks….

Dennis Kneale, *Wall Street Journal (Martin, 2003)*

Journalism: a profession whose business is to explain to others what it does not personally understand.

Lord Northcliffe, *The Mirror* and *Mail* Proprietor

No-one expects PR people to know all the answers. But we do expect them to know who in the client company will know the answer and be able to pass it on verbatim.

Barry Fox, *New Scientist*

Not everyone realises that to write a really good piece of journalism is at least as intellectually demanding as the achievement of any scholar.

Max Weber, Political Economist *(Weber, 1918)*

The words, pictures and graphics that are the stuff of journalism have to be brilliantly packaged – they must feed the mind and move the heart.

Rupert Murdoch, Proprietor, News International *(Brook, 2006)*

The press is a defence against tyranny, corruption and injustice … a source of light, shining into the dark places where the powerful and corrupt want to keep things hidden.

Alexander Lebedev, Proprietor, *Standard (Robinson, 2010)*

A carnival of insecurity.

Andrew Marr, *'My Trade' (2004)*

Journalists aren't supposed to praise things. It's a violation of work rules almost as serious as buying drinks with our own money.

P J O'Rourke, *Rolling Stone, Washington Post et al. (O'Rourke, 1992)*

REFERENCES

Barber, L. (1998). *Demon Barber*. New York, NY: Viking.

Brook, S. (2006, March 13). Murdoch looks into the crystal ball. *The Guardian*. Retrieved from https://www.theguardian.com/technology/2006/mar/13/news.rupertmurdoch1. Accessed on August 2018.

Davies, N. (2008). *Flat earth news: An award-winning reporter exposes falsehood, distortion and propaganda in the global media*. London: Chatto.

Davies, N. (2015). *Hack attack: How the truth caught up with Rupert Murdoch*. London: Random House.

Kelner, S. (2016, July 11). The booing of David Cameron revealed a boorish revolution. *iNews*. Retrieved from https://inews.co.uk/opinion/columnists/booing-cameron-revealed-boorish-revolution/. Accessed on August 2018.

Marr, A. (2004). *My trade: A short history of British Journalism*. London: MacMillan.

Martin, D. (2003, October). Gilded and Gelded: Hard-Won lessons from the PR wars. *Harvard Business Review*. Retrieved from https://hbr.org/2003/10/gilded-and-gelded-hard-won-lessons-from-the-pr-wars. Accessed on August 2018.

Neeley, L. (2012, September 12). Taming beastly press releases. *Compass*. Retrieved from https://www.compassscicomm.org/single-post/2017/04/14/Taming-Beastly-Press-Releases. Accessed on August 2018.

O'Rourke, P. J. (1992). *Give war a chance*. London: Pan MacMillan.

Robinson, J. (2010, November 14). Alexander Lebedev vows to continue fight against 'tyranny'. *The Guardian*. Retrieved from https://www.theguardian.com/media/2010/nov/14/alexander-lebedev-tyranny-independent. Accessed on August 2018.

The Guardian. (2018, May 26). 'Our human response is vital': Snapshot of life as a picture editor. *The Guardian*. Retrieved from https://www.theguardian.com/artanddesign/2018/may/26/our-human-response-is-vital-snapshot-of-life-as-a-picture-editor. Accessed on August 2018.

Weber, M. (1918). *New York Times*.

Wolff, M. (2010). *Autumn of the Moguls: My misadventures with the titans, poseurs, and money guys who mastered and messed up big media*. London: Harper Collins.

Zinsser, W. K. (2006). *On writing well: An informal guide to writing nonfiction*. London: Harper Collins.

INDEX